Uncle Russell AND Daddy Stories

Colin D. Standish

Cover design and layout
Greg Solie • AltamontGraphics.com

Text editing and layout
Harvey Steck

Published by
Hartland Publications
PO Box 1, Rapidan, VA, 22733 USA
(540) 672-3566
Printed in USA

ISBN #0-923309-24-1

Contents

Chapter 1

Story Time

The stories retold in this book are for children and young people—and of course fathers and mothers. They are selected from the many stories I told my children Nigel and Alexandra as they were growing up.

Because of the heavy responsibilities which I had in the administration of Hartland Institute, the frequent weekend preaching appointments, and the overseas trips which I made a number of times each year, I did everything to be a responsible father in these circumstances to the children whom God had entrusted to us.

Every morning and evening we would have family worship. In their early life it would consist of special scripture songs and other children's hymns and reading through with the children *My Bible Friends* and Arthur Maxwell's volumes of *The Bible Story*. Of course, when I was away, my dear wife Cheryl was responsible for leading out. As they grew a little older, we added memory texts to our worships. We began to realize how our own ability to memorize, as we were advancing in years, was far below the speed with which our children were able to memorize, even at young ages such as six and seven. It was another reminder to us how important it is to teach the memorization of the Scriptures to boys and girls from their earliest years. We also began to involve the children in the prayers and lead them to help in the worships. Of course, as they got older, we also gave them the opportunity to do some of the reading.

Further, I also felt a great burden to be with my children as they were tucked into bed, and before I would have a final prayer with them,

I would tell them stories. Over a number of years, I especially concentrated on what I called the "Uncle Russell and Daddy stories"—stories from the childhood and youth of my twin brother and me. I sought to bring home some of the lessons to be learned from these stories.

Years later, Alexandra, approaching her eighteenth birthday, urged me to write up the Uncle Russell and Daddy stories. At first, I was a little reluctant, but as I contemplated the request, I thought they might be interesting and helpful to other children as they realize the way in which God was to bless us and to guide us through the difficulties and the struggles of childhood and early adolescent.

So, here is the book. I pray that every boy and girl and teenager will be greatly blessed and learn some of the lessons which we learned in our childhood and youth. I pray each one, including the parents who may read this book, will gain spiritual blessings and courage. Above all, I pray that each one will be ready for Jesus when He comes to take home His faithful ones. That is my deepest prayer.

Chapter 2

Daddy's Boy

When Mummy and Daddy had been married for many years, we began to talk about the possibility of adopting a child because we had no children of our own. However, the years quickly passed by, and Daddy was eventually more than 40 years of age, and that excluded us by regulations from being provided with an adoption from the state agencies. This left Mummy and Daddy with one and only one option, and that was to adopt privately.

In the United States it is very difficult to adopt children. There are so many couples seeking adoptions and so few children available for adoption. This has resulted from the fact that there are so many abortions on the one hand and, on the other hand, the fact that single parents are increasingly deciding to keep their babies, even though so many of them are not able to provide a stable home for them. By the time that we were ministering at Weimar Institute, in Northern California, every time Daddy would preach somewhere, Mummy would say, "If there is any doctor at your meetings, ask him if he can help us to find an adoption." I explained to Mother that most of the doctors which I would meet would have no opportunity to help with an adoption because they were not obstetricians and as such would not have any knowledge of babies available for adoption. Often there were one or more doctors at the meetings, and I would inquire, but always with the same results. I had almost come to the idea that it would be impossible to find an adoption.

Then we heard that there were two children—one ten month old baby girl from Honduras and one one-month-old baby boy from Guatemala—who were available for adoption. We thought this was a wonderful answer to our prayers. We traveled to the Immigration Department in San Francisco where we were told that because we were not American citizens we could not adopt foreign children. We thought that was strange. Yet they made it plain that even though we were foreigners we could adopt American children. We wondered why it was not the other way around. However, it would seem that the Immigration and Naturalization Service was concerned that foreigners would bring in many adoptees to sell them on the black market to make money. Now we were left with the only remaining option—to find, if at all possible, a private adoption in the United States.

God worked a marvelous miracle, Nigel, for us to be able to adopt you into our family. In 1981 Elder Thomas Nesland, a departmental director of the Southern California Conference, telephoned Daddy, asking me if I would be available to speak at the five-day Campers' camp meeting at Frazier Park in Southern California over the July fourth weekend in 1982. This had been a small camp meeting started some years before by earnest, faithful Seventh-day Adventists. Many would come in their RVs and campers; some brought tents; and some conference tents were pitched for those who did not have their own accommodations. By the time Daddy was approached to speak there, about 500 came each camp meeting. Daddy said he certainly was willing to come, and Elder Nesland responded that he would get back to Daddy if things worked out. When, after several months, he did not contact Daddy again, Daddy thought that he had decided to bring other speakers.

Soon after we had arrived in Australia on furlough at the end of 1981, Daddy heard from his secretary that Elder Morgan, the president of the Ontario Conference in Canada, had invited him to be one of the main speakers at the Ontario camp meeting. Daddy was delighted for that invitation because I had already preached for Elder Morgan in 1977 at the Indiana camp meeting, and Elder Morgan had appreciated the impact which Daddy had made at that camp meeting, especially upon the youth. Daddy quickly communicated with his secretary and informed her that certainly Daddy would make himself available for that camp meeting.

Mummy and Daddy decided that they would take their vacation and drive across America to the camp meeting, seeing some of the wonderful natural sights along the way. Daddy had not done that, although Mummy had seen some of these sites when she had first traveled to Weimar with "Auntie Vickie." We especially planned to see Yellowstone National Park.

When we arrived back to Weimar from Australia in February, Daddy casually asked his secretary if everything was finalized for me to attend the camp meeting in Ontario. Her response shocked Daddy, "Oh, no, I cancelled you out of those meetings." In astonishment Daddy asked her "Why?" "Well," she said, "Someone called me from Southern California and said you had promised to speak at another camp meeting which was to be held at the same period of time." Daddy said, "I would never have chosen the Campers' camp meeting."

The Campers' camp meeting was small—about 500 people meeting for five days. At the camp meeting in Ontario several thousand people would attend for nine or ten days. Daddy was startled that his secretary would cancel him out without first contacting him. A simple phone call was all that would have been needed. When Daddy told Mummy she was very upset; so much so that Daddy had to remind her, "Love, all things work together for good to them that love the Lord." Mummy responded by saying, "That is what you always say." Daddy reminded her that it was not what Daddy had said but what the Word of Scripture said. Little did Daddy and Mummy know that God was working His plan for us to adopt the yet unborn child who would eventually become our dear son, Nigel. In spite of everything, Daddy and Mummy had a fine time at the Campers' camp meeting with many earnest Seventh-day Adventists from Southern California.

Mummy had been so persistent seeking the possibility of a private adoption, but it seemed almost impossible. However, while at the Campers' camp meeting, Mummy was walking with Mrs. Marilyn Hanson, the wife of Dr. Deone Hanson. We had met them for the first time earlier in 1982 on our return from Australia when Daddy had preached at Ontario church pastored by Elder James Wolter (who is now a member of the Hartland Institute board). As they were walking, Mrs. Hanson saw some distance away a young physician, Dr. Elizabeth Iskander. Dr. Iskander was not practicing medicine at this time because she was caring for her two young sons. However, Mrs. Hanson knew that her husband was a very popular obstetrician at the Glendale Adventist Hospital. Therefore, Mrs. Hanson called to Dr. Iskander and said, "The Standishes are desirous of adopting a child. Your husband is an obstetrician. Would you see if it is possible for him to obtain an adoption for the Standishes?" Dr. Iskander indicated that she would try her best. However, when Mummy told Daddy of the brief conversation, he thought it was most unlikely that anything would eventuate from the brief contact. After all, the obstetrician did not know us, and, as we were to learn later, he told his wife it was very difficult for him to find adoptions even for women who were his patients who found great difficulty in having children.

Shortly after the camp meeting, Mummy and Daddy traveled to Crieff, in Scotland, as at the time there was a health institution operated by Seventh-day Adventists in that city. There were some difficulties in conducting this institution, and Weimar had been asked if they would consider taking it over. We were overjoyed to join two other Weimar administrators to look over that possibility. It did not work out for Weimar to take over this institution. On the way home Daddy had arranged to stop at Hamburg, Pennsylvania, where Charles Wheeling was conducting a seminar on end-time events at Blue Mountain Academy. Mummy journeyed on to Washington, D. C. to meet with some of our friends whom we had made while I was president of Columbia Union College.

After arriving at Hamburg, staying with Mr. and Mrs. Richard Mayer at their nursing home, Daddy received a telephone message from Professor Francis Cosentine, the director of admissions at Weimar College, explaining that Dr. Elizabeth Iskander had called and that Daddy was to get in touch with her. Daddy was not familiar with the name, but he called the telephone number he had been given.

When Daddy telephoned Dr. Elizabeth, she very quickly came to the point, "Are you still desirous of adopting a child?" Well Daddy remembers his response, "Yes, we are. Especially my wife is." Then she said, "My husband has a patient who is expecting a child about September

10, and he would be willing to arrange for you to adopt the child once it is born. However, the child's father is an American Indian. Will that make any difference?" Daddy assured her it would not because we had already been willing to adopt two children from Central America who would have had American Indian background."

Daddy immediately called Mummy. She was very excited and called Dr. Elizabeth Iskander and spent much time discussing the matter with her. It was especially exciting to us, for we learned that the expected birth was only a month and one-half away. We had absolutely nothing prepared. Normally parents, after realizing that the mother-to-be is expecting a baby, have at least seven months to prepare. But that was not the case for Mummy and Daddy.

Later we learned that this unborn child (which at that time we did not know whether it would be a boy or a girl) had been offered to a family, and they had accepted the responsibility of adopting this child. However, not long after they had accepted, they had withdrawn because the husband had a heart attack, and the wife had to enter hospital for major surgery. They knew then that they were not in a position to take this added responsibility.

Then the baby was offered to the daughter of the administrator of the Glendale Adventist Hospital. She decided not to adopt this child. We believe it was because she was told that the father of this yet unborn child was American Indian. Probably she decided she did not want to adopt a child of mixed blood. What a surprise it was to us to find out when you were born that your father was not an American Indian! God had preserved you to be a part of our family.

As September arrived we were eagerly waiting, hoping that there would be no change in the intention of the mother to offer her babe for adoption. Indeed Daddy and Mummy did not have to wait long because on September 3, we received the exciting word that you had just been born that Friday afternoon at about 4:00 p.m. Mummy's excitement and joy was very great. Even though you were born one week before we had expected your birth, it was obvious that you were a full-term baby because you were eight pound two ounces. Of course, we also learned that you were a little boy.

Immediately we called and booked a flight for Mummy to fly from Sacramento to Burbank airport. Dr. Elizabeth Iskander promised to be at the airport to pick Mummy up and take her to the Glendale Hospital, which she did.

When you were just seventeen hours old Mummy took you from the hospital. It was Sabbath morning. Mummy had no suitable clothes for you, but she wrapped you in a blanket, and on Sunday, Mother, Auntie Vickie, and Aunt Luce (Mrs. Walters—no relation to Auntie Vickie) purchased clothes for you—the first you ever "owned." Later on Sunday, Mummy took you to a wedding of our West Indian friends in Southern California, and you can imagine what a center of attention you were. Like most very young babies, you spent considerable time crying when you were not sleeping or eating. Mummy quickly purchased baby formula for you.

On your fourth day of life Mummy booked a flight to bring you back to Sacramento. We learned late that the rules were that babies were not permitted to travel by plane until they were at least ten days old. However, no one questioned your age, and Mummy did bring you home. Daddy drove down from Weimar to the Sacramento airport to see his newborn son for the first time. Eventually Mummy came down the escalator to the baggage area. In her arms was our little boy who was immediately placed in Daddy's arms, and Daddy could not believe it. Here was a little, fair boy—not the little dark skinned boy which Daddy had expected, thinking that you would be part American Indian.

When we took you the 50 miles back to Weimar, east of the Sacramento airport, you can imagine the excitement of the people, especially the women and the girls, anxious to catch a glimpse of this little baby boy. However, only God knew the miracles He had worked for you to become our first-born child.

1. If Daddy and Mummy had gone to Ontario camp meeting instead of the Campers' camp meeting, which we both desired to do, you would never have become our son.

2. Had Mrs. Hansen not seen Dr. Elizabeth Iskander at the Campers' camp meeting you would not have been our boy.
3. If the first couple who had accepted you had not become ill, you would not have been our child.
4. If the daughter of the Glendale Adventist Hospital Administrator had not been told that your father was American Indian, we believe that you would not have been our son.

This is how we knew of a certainty that God had brought you into our family. When we had discussed the possibility of adopting a child, Daddy began to pray regularly, "Dear Lord; do not allow us to adopt any children unless we can bring them up for the kingdom of Heaven."

Nigel, you were dedicated to the Lord twice: first by Elder Wendell Wilcox, the godly minister of the Colfax church, five miles east of Weimar, and also in Southern California by Pastor Hilbert Nembhard. Pastor Nembhard was the chairman of the religion department when Daddy was president of West Indies College in Jamaica.

How happy we were when we received word that your adoption could be finalized at the Auburn Courthouse in California, July 8, 1983! With a couple of friends we drove to the courthouse and eventually were ushered into the office of the judge. The judge reminded us that the adoption was not something about which we could change our minds later and, of course, we had no intention of doing this. We were so very happy to have our son.

Eventually, we signed the documents, and you were officially Nigel Richard Standish. What a proud and happy moment that was! Sadly, immediately after your adoption had taken place, the judge had to proceed to the courtroom to lead out in a trial of two thirteen-year-old girls who were charged with the murder of an elderly lady in Auburn whom they had robbed. We moved away from Weimar before hearing the results of the trial.

We did not leave immediately, however, because Daddy had an appointment to preach at a camp by a lake in northern California to a group of faithful people. Then it was on our way to Hartland. We stopped at a number of the wonderful sights on the way, such as Yellowstone National Park and the presidential monuments in South Dakota's Black Hills. I also preached in Minneapolis.

Before we were half way across the continent you became sick. Mummy telephoned Dr. Lloyd Pratt in Sacramento, and fortunately you soon recovered. We arrived at Hartland July 26, 1983. One week later you began to walk just before you turned eleven months old.

It has been a wonderful blessing for Daddy and Mummy to have our son, and we look to the future to see what God will accomplish through your ministry for Him. You are truly a special gift from the Lord.

A wise son maketh a glad father. . . . Proverbs 10:1

Chapter 3

Daddy's Girl

We had been greatly blessed by the providential adoption of Nigel. We wondered if it would be in God's plan for us to find a second child for adoption. God also had a plan for our little daughter, but we knew nothing about that plan. From time to time Mummy and Daddy had talked about our desire to adopt a second child; however, it seemed unlikely that we would ever succeed.

While Nigel was still a few months old, we were approached about adopting two little children who had come from a very poor home. We decided against that adoption because we knew that it would be very difficult, since the children were not newborns, and we were having many sleepless nights with Nigel because of a severe case of colic. Sometimes Daddy would be up five times a night trying to help his boy, who was screaming because of severe pain. Mother often would not be able to help much because she was not well, and so, on a few occasions, Mrs. Jesse Taylor would take Nigel to give us the chance of a good night's sleep, which was a great blessing to us.

There were times when we thought that another adoption would never happen. However, as God so wonderfully works, the door was opened at a time when we were least expecting it. Daddy was preaching at the Cape Cod church in Massachusetts. We were staying at the home of Dr. and Mrs. Ed Lattimer. For many years Dr. Lattimer had been a wonderfully dedicated physician at the New England Memorial Hospital in Boston. As the Lattimers lived very close to the home of the famous Kennedy family, they took us to view the Kennedy homes in Hyannis.

On the Saturday night after our Sabbath meetings, we were talking together when the telephone rang. To our great surprise the telephone call was for Daddy. It was from a woman in Sacramento named Mrs. Eleanor Morrison, with whom we had become very good friends while serving at Weimar. She was a fine Christian woman, and, after greeting me, she inquired as to whether or not we were still interested in a second adoption. Daddy told her we certainly were, and he passed the phone to Mummy. Mrs. Morrison then explained that her daughter was nursing in the Redlands Community Hospital in Southern California. One of the other nurses had shared with her the fact that her younger sister was soon to have a child, and at that point in time they had no decision as to whom to adopt the child, which had already been determined to be a girl. It was only a short time before the due date for your birth.

We were then put in touch with the family, who actually lived in New Mexico. The mother-to-be had come to California and was staying with her sister, Leanne, who was nursing at the Redlands Community Hospital. Mummy spent a long time on the phone with the mother (your biological grandmother) of the young lady. Because the family members, like Nigel's mother, were Roman Catholic, they desired that their child be adopted to a Roman Catholic family. She traveled to California to stay with her older sister who was working hard to help finance her husband who was training in the medical field. Twice they telephoned the Roman Catholic adoption, agency asking the agency to send the papers to take the child to adopt her into a Roman Catholic home. For some reason, on neither occasion did they receive a response from the Catholic adoption agency. This was amazing because such agencies are eager to find adoptions for the many couples who are seeking children for adoption. You can see how God worked marvelously on your behalf.

However, God had His plans for our little girl. Once again he was working His miraculous ways that we might have a second child in our family—one whom we could bring up for the kingdom of God and for the service of the Lord.

It was at this point that the family was very anxious about where they would place the soon-to-be-born child. The grandmother was very concerned about the kind of home to which the baby would be adopted, and a number of times she talked with Mummy, asking her questions such as, "What do Seventh-day Adventists believe?" "Are they Christians?" Mother told her that I was a Seventh-day Adventist minister. She asked what religious training you would be given. Mummy explained that we had family worship morning and evening and that we had already adopted one child and that we attended church every week.

The grandmother then desired to know what kind of education we would give to the child. Mummy responded that we would, for the first years of your schooling, home-school you. However, she was told that we had a little school at Hartland which eventually you would attend. The grandmother of the expectant woman said she thought that would be good. Then she asked concerning what kind of diet we would give to the child. Mummy told her that we were vegans. It would seem that Mummy's answers could have been interpreted as fanatical, and the grandmother could have decided to find another home for you. However, that did not happen. Finally she said she would consult the family to make a decision. After several days the grandmother called back to say they had made a decision that when the baby was born she would be available for us to adopt into our family. We were filled with great joy. We explained to three-year-old Nigel that he soon would have an adopted sister. He seemed very intrigued with this and seemed to look forward to seeing his sister.

Eventually on September 30, 1985, Daddy received a phone call in his office at Hartland Institute and it was from Leanne, the sister of your birth mother, and with a very happy voice she said, "Congratulations! You now have a daughter." Immediately Mother and Nigel made plans to travel to California to bring our baby back to Hartland. The family decided to have you "baptized" (sprinkled) by the priest before they would permit you to leave the hospital. The priest refused to "baptize" you because you were being adopted to a Protestant family, so the family themselves sprinkled water on the your forehead and christened you Teresa Marie.

One day after you were born, Mummy met your birth mother and fed you in the hospital. The second day, Mummy took you from the hospital, ready to bring you back to Virginia very quickly, but there soon developed a great problem. Daddy had telephoned the Virginia Social Services, and they explained to me that because of the laws of Virginia, we were not eligible to adopt you. The law said that if there had been anyone involved in a private adoption other than the mother of the child herself, then the adoption could not be completed. No doubt this was a law meant to stop black-market trading in babies. However, that was the last thought in our minds, as Social Services knew.

The Madison County Social Services officer had come to our home before you were born, inspected it, talked with us, and she had been most favorable. She had said, "What a delight it is to come to Hartland now and see the difference from before it was purchased by your people!" Itinerant people had lived on the property and she had had to investigate family disputes and child abuse. Now it was a joy for her to come for adoptions.

I called the State Attorney General's Department in Richmond. The officer with whom I spoke was very sympathetic. He agreed that we had had an excellent report from the Social Services and, as he put it, "You are being hurt by a technicality." I asked him what we could do. He said, "The only thing I can suggest is that you hire a lawyer to work with you." We had hoped not to have to employ a lawyer because that had cost us a lot of money in Sacramento with Nigel's adoption, and we felt we knew enough ourselves now how to do the adoption without a lawyer. Now we realized we needed a lawyer.

In the end Daddy spoke with a lady lawyer from Orange, and she agreed to take the case and work to see what she could do to help us. In the meantime, Mummy, Nigel and you were still in California, staying with Aunt Vickie. The weeks started to pass by. We were afraid to bring you back to Virginia in case you would be taken from us by the Social Services Department. Mummy called the Social Services Department in Sacramento, and they were most upset with the approach taken by Virginia. They pointed out that you were born in California, and therefore you were their baby to adopt. The Director of Social Services in California called the Director in Richmond, Virginia, but was told there was nothing which could be done because of the laws in the Commonwealth of Virginia. The Director of Social Services in California became very angry, but that did not help in the situation. Thus it seemed we could do nothing.

In the meantime, from time to time, Daddy would telephone to Mummy and once, when I was talking to Nigel he said, "Daddy, when will I see you again? It's a long day since I last saw you." Daddy assured him I hoped that that would not be too long.

I thought to bring the family back to the District of Columbia where you would be safe, because the District of Columbia had reciprocity with the state of California; therefore, there would bc no problem for you to be there. However, after about eight weeks, Daddy telephoned again to the Attorney General's Department in Virginia. The officer assured me that if we were to bring our baby back to Virginia you would not be taken from us. That was good news, and very quickly Mummy, Nigel and little daughter Alexandra came back, and I saw you and held you for the very first time.

Once again Mummy and Daddy were confident that God would be our help because we knew God had guided this far, but we did not know how it would happen. All this time, as in the case of Nigel, the parents could have taken you back at any time. It would have been heartbreaking to us if this were to happen; yet we saw the mighty hand of God working, and we did not lose courage. From time to time we talked to our lawyer. On one occasion she said, "Perhaps there is a judge who would take the intent of the law rather than the letter of the law." However because the judge in our district at that time was Judge Sullenberger, who had been one of the attorneys who had helped us to purchase Hartland property, she felt that he would follow the letter of the law and therefore would not give assent to the adoption. She suggested that we wait until the judge was either sick or gone on vacation. Possibly the judge sitting for him during his absence would be more considerate of our situation.

Months passed by, and when you were more than eleven months old, the attorney called Daddy excitedly. She had been talking with a lawyer in Fredericksburg about your case. This lawyer had learned that there had been a "tag-on" to a major bill which had passed the Virginia State House in which the law was changed to permit that, if there was no reason other than the fact that a person other than the mother had contacted us, then the adoption could be granted. You can imagine how thrilled Mummy and Daddy were when we heard this!

Quickly our lawyer placed the case before Judge Sullenberger. We did not attend the hearing as we had had to attend in California for Nigel's adoption. Things were done much differently in Virginia. Judge Sullenberger affirmed the adoption, and we were conscious again of God's leadings. However, according to Virginia law, there would still be a six-month's delay period before the adoption would become final. This was an opportunity for your genetic family to take you back if they so chose.

Alexandra, on your first birthday we received a gift of a lovely dress for you, sent by your birth mother, with a note in which she said how much she loved you. Once again, we realized that God had worked in a wonderful way for us to bring you into our family, and we know that He has a mighty work for you also as for Nigel as you both follow the leading of the Lord. When, on March 10, 1987, the adoption was finalized, Mummy and Daddy and little Nigel were very happy indeed. It had taken seventeen months and ten days from your birth to the finalization of your adoption. You have been such a joy to Mummy and Daddy.

We had already dedicated you to the Lord at the Vision Valley (Sydney, Australia) meetings conducted by Hartland in November, 1986. You were dedicated to the Lord and His service by Pastor George Burnside, the dedicated New Zealand evangelist.

We look to the future to witness the Lord's ministry through your life as you follow God's divine calling. Mummy and Daddy often think of the wonderful providence of God which led you and Nigel to become precious members of our family. How different your lives would have been had you been adopted to worldly Roman Catholic families! God truly chose you for our family! We appreciate how much you love each other. God is honoring our prayers to prepare you for His heavenly kingdom. If God chooses you to marry, we pray you will be married to godly, dedicated young people.

Mummy and Daddy are so happy that both of you are baptized members of the Seventh-day Adventist Church and that you love serving Him and working for the salvation of others.

> Many daughters have done virtuously, but thou excellest them all. Proverbs 31:29

Chapter 4

Learning About Our Forebears

When Uncle Russell and Daddy were little boys, we loved to hear how our family became Seventh-day Adventists. Most of what we learned came from Grandma, as she communicated more than Grandpa on family issues.

The first member of our family to become a Seventh-day Adventist was Great-grandma Bailey. She had come to Australia with her parents from Newcastle, England, to Newcastle, Australia, in 1880, when she was nine years of age. She was only fifteen when she married Great-grandpa John Bailey, who was then twenty. However, she was a very godly woman and was a member of the Primitive Methodist Church, where she attended regularly every Sunday. In 1899, she received a tract in her letterbox which she eagerly read, for she received very little spiritual material to read. The same morning the following week was a second tract, and the third week again. Anxious to find out who was distributing the tracts, Great-grandma decided the next week that she would stand by the door, waiting to see who would come at night to put another tract in her letterbox.

Sure enough, in the dim light of the gas lamps which lit the streets in those days, she saw someone coming and as he approached her letterbox, she moved out quickly, and found it was a seventeen-year-old, shy youth, who was distributing these tracts. She told him how much she had been enjoying them, and he was wise enough to ask her if she would like a lady to come to study the Bible with her. Great-grandma Bailey thought that would be wonderful, especially as her husband had shown no interest in Christianity other than his deep hatred of Roman Catholics.

Great-grandma Bailey studied eagerly with this lady Bible worker, but eventually she was confronted with the Sabbath truth. This was an entirely new understanding for her, but because she believed everything in the Bible to be true, she eventually realized she had to make the step. What a big step this was! She had not even heard of Seventh-day Adventists before meeting this lady Bible worker. She was then 28 years of age and had six children. Grandma was still more than twelve years away from being born, for she was the last of eleven children. However, Great-grandma made the right decision, and the next Sabbath she prepared her children to go to church.

Great-grandpa was quite shocked. He knew nothing about the Bible studies, nor about her new convictions on the Sabbath, and he wondered where she was going. She just simply said she was going to church. He thought it was strange; however, the next week when she was doing the same, he became alarmed and said, "They will have you going to church every day of the week," because at this time, she was still continuing to attend the Primitive Methodist Church on Sunday as well.

The next week, Great-grandpa demanded, "What is going on?" Great-grandma realized that she could not hide the situation any longer, and she tried to explain that she had discovered that the real Sabbath day was the seventh day of the week. Great-grandpa barely tolerated her going to church every week, but to have such a fanatical view that he had never heard before was more than he could tolerate. With great passion for which he was frequently known, he shouted, "I demand that you stop going to that church!" Great-grandma had been used to yielding to the strong-willed demands of her husband, but now she was under deep conviction and she turned to him and said, "John, all these years I have tried to do everything to please you, but on this, I have to follow God." He was not used to his wife questioning any of his commands, and it would appear that he did not quite know how to respond. After sometime, he got used to her Sabbath observance, and of course, no longer did she continue to attend the Primitive Methodist Church.

Great-grandma Bailey did not have to learn how to keep the Sabbath holy, because she had been attempting to keep Sunday holy the way Sabbath should be kept, as was not uncommon in those days. The Hamilton Seventh-day Adventist Church in Newcastle, where Uncle Russell and Daddy were baptized many years later, had been built in 1899. In 1900 Great-grandma Bailey was baptized into the Seventh-day Adventist Church, and later Grandma Standish would be baptized there as a teenager, as well as Great-auntie Amy and Great-auntie Vera before her, and we believe also Great-auntie Alice, although she was later to stray from God's church. As far as we know, none of your great-uncles ever showed a real interest in the Seventh-day Adventist faith, and that is very sad. Great-grandma Bailey remained a faithful Seventh-day Adventist for the rest of her life, and we certainly hope to meet her in the heavenly kingdom.

The conversion of Great-grandpa Bailey in his old age was one of the greatest miracles which Uncle Russell and Daddy have ever seen. He was such a tough man, who saw ministers as parasites on society. He showed no respect for them, and he hardly knew what the inside of a church looked like. After his birth in 1865, he grew up in Australia in an obviously hardened, anti-Catholic, Irish-Protestant home. His only passion which had anything to do with religion was to hate those "tykes," the term he most commonly used for Roman Catholics.

Great-grandma Bailey died in October of 1942, without seeing the slightest evidence of the response of her husband of 56 years to any form of Christianity, let alone the Seventh-day Adventist faith. However, as Grandma and Grandpa, with Uncle Russell and Daddy, moved in to live with Great-grandpa, he began to talk very lovingly about his wife, and sometimes very remorseful of how he treated her. We began to hear him say, "I just want to be where Alice will be."

Grandma, seeing the softness of his heart, contacted the then pastor in the Newcastle district, Pastor O.K. Anderson, and asked if he would come to help Great-grandpa Bailey to accept the Lord. These studies did lead to the conversion of Great-grandpa Bailey.

Great-grandpa and Great-grandma are buried together in the Sandgate Cemetery in Newcastle. Uncle Russell and Daddy hope they can introduce you to them even before we get to heaven as we travel with Jesus back to the heavenly home.

> And I heard a voice from heaven saying unto me, Write, Blessed are the dead which die in the Lord from henceforth: Yea, saith the Spirit, that they may rest from their labours; and their works do follow them. Revelation 14:13

Chapter 5

Grandpa's Family Learn about the Seventh-day Adventist Faith

Much of what we know about Grandpa's background came from Grandma, some of Grandpa's relatives, and some from our own research. Grandpa had two strands of immigrant forebears to Australia—first from England and secondly from Eastern Germany. At the end of the 1840s, both came to Australia, and both landed in South Australia. It was then a new colony, first established in 1836.

Your Great-great-great-grandfather Thomas Standish came out from England, apparently on a boat which carried many German immigrants. He was the son of a Knight of the realm—Sir William Standish, who would be your Great-great-great-great-grandfather. He lived in Warwickshire, a county of England. He sent his two sons to officer military training school, but both greatly disliked the training, and they left without authorization. In those days that was a very serious offense, so they quickly emigrated to Australia to avoid punishment.

In Australia, Great-great-great-grandfather Thomas married a German lady about twelve years older than he was. He was 23 and she was 35. In those days, the number of women in the new colony was small compared with men. No doubt, this was part of the reason for what seemed an unusual marriage. They had four sons, including Great-great-grandfather Samuel David Standish, their second son. Daddy's second name was called after his second name. He also married a German because they were living in the Barossa valley, which had become the home for many Germans. This valley was about 50 miles north of Adelaide. These Germans became the major wine growers of Australia—not an industry we admire.

They had lived in the Prussian part of Germany, in the province of Selicia, which is now part of Poland. They had opposed the Emperor Fredrick Wilhelm II, who was bringing Calvin concepts into the Lutheran Church, especially in respect of the communion service.

While we agree with the emperor's beliefs, we do admire our forebears for standing for what they believe to be the truth. However, Martin Luther was wrong on the issue. Luther taught a strange concept of consubstantiation, which was not very far away from the Roman Catholic concept of transubstantiation, which taught that the priest actually recreated Christ in the wafer used in the communion mass.

They were persecuted for opposing the emperor. Their leader, Pastor August L.C. Kaval, met William Angas, who convinced these Germans against migrating to the Ukraine where they had been planning to go to avoid the conflict with the emperor, but to go to Australia, and this they did. The group included your Great-great-great-great-grandmother Maria Rosina Heider, her three daughters, and two sons-in-law. The only unmarried daughter became your Great-great-grandmother, Anna Elizabeth Heider. The settlers lived very simply and with little income. However, no doubt, most of the other people lived the same way. The family became staunch Reformed Lutheran members, and remained that way until 1915.

A tragedy occurred in 1915 when Great-great-grandpa Samuel Standish lost his wife Pauline Bertha Schulz. She had come down with a heavy flu. The doctor came to treat her, and he gave her what he said was a "very strong medicine." Within two hours after she took the medicine, she died following convulsions. No doubt, it was a deadly poison which he had given to her. She was in her 50s at the time.

It was six months later that the Seventh-day Adventists decided to send a layman, Brother Bachaus, into the Barossa Valley to witness to the Germans. This layman had much success, and in a short period of time a number of the German families had accepted the Seventh-day Adventist faith. This included the Standish family, one of the very few in that valley who had an English name. Keep in mind that our forebears spoke German as their first language, even though they had an English name. Others in the region became Seventh-day Adventists, including the Kranz, Zaunet, Maywald, Klix, Rathel, Wagner, and Roennfeldt families. These families became the early members of the Nuriupta church, some of whose children became very important Seventh-day Adventist workers and leaders. Some of our family members told us that they wonder if Great-great-grandfather Samuel David Standish would have become a Seventh-day Adventist had his wife still been alive. Apparently she was a very strong woman, and would have done everything to stop him if she did not accept the Seventh-day Adventist message.

However, God certainly made him a faithful Seventh-day Adventist. He had been a deacon in the Lutheran church in Tunanda, another town about four and a half miles from where he lived. How grateful we are that he took such a stand! Grandpa was about three years old when a number of the members of the family joined the Seventh-day Adventist Church. As with Great-grandma Bailey, Great-great-grandfather Standish did not have to learn how to keep holy the Sabbath day, because he had kept Sunday holy in the same way as we keep the Sabbath holy.

We were to meet Great-great-grandpa Standish only once when we were about three or four years of age, but we still remember the huge beard which he had. He died before he reached his 81st birthday, and had been faithful to Jesus all those years. God has given you both a very strong heritage and a faithful heritage in the family's past history.

Chapter 6

The Birth of Uncle Russell and Daddy

Grandpa Standish and Grandma Standish had met at Avondale College in 1932. They were married in September of that year by Pastor Giliard, a well known minister at that time. Because they had no money for a wedding, the wedding service was a simple one held in the home of Great-grandpa and Great-grandma Bailey, Grandma's parents. It was very difficult for them, for Grandpa had no job, as was true of many men in Australia because those were the depression years. He did get a little dole, which was money from the government for men out of work, and he did earn some money every now and again from digging with a pick and shovel in a gravel pit.

Grandpa and Grandma could not afford to live in a home of their own, so they lived with Great-grandma and Great-grandpa. However, when things became difficult at the home, they traveled to Great-grandpa's home in Vine Vale in the Barossa Valley of South Australia, about 50 miles north of Adelaide, the state capital of South Australia. At least when they were there, there was work which they could do. By April, in the early Autumn, they were able to pick grapes, for this was the grape-growing capital of Australia. However, by this time Grandma was pregnant, and the work was hard and the days were long. She had much trouble with pain in her back, but they were able to earn a little money, small though it was.

A sad experience had happened in February of 1933, five months after they had married. One of Grandma's brothers, Great-uncle Cecil, then 33 years of age, was a tram conductor. In those days the trams were built so that the conductor collecting the fares had to move along a tiny platform outside the trams and lean into the carriage to take fares. That day, which happened to be a Sabbath day, Great-uncle Cecil was collecting fares. It was a rainy day and maybe the platform was slippery. Whatever happened, he fell off the tram as it was chugging along, hit his head on the roadway, and died a few hours later in hospital.

Before Grandma gave birth, Grandpa and Grandma returned to Hamilton in Newcastle, New South Wales. About three weeks before it was expected for Grandma to give birth, she realized she was soon to have her baby. She walked with Grandpa to a two-story home in Lawson Street, Hamilton, only five and half blocks from where they lived and half a block from the Seventh-day Adventist church. This was a two-story house where hospital care was given and babies were born. Not long before the birth, Grandma was told the startling possibility that there may be twins—something she had never considered. When the birth took place it was true; twins were born to the great delight of Grandma. However, she was wholly unprepared for two children.

They had chosen names for either a boy or a girl, not knowing which would be born, but if the birth was a boy then they had decided to call him Colin David. Colin was a name they liked, and David was chosen because it was the second name of Great-great-grandpa Standish (Samuel David Standish), who had had to act as Grandpa's father in his growing-up days. Daddy was the first to be born so he was named Colin David. About twenty minutes later, Uncle Russell was born, and he was finally named Russell Roland, Roland being the second name of Grandpa (Darcy Roland Standish). The attending nurse had put a ribbon around Daddy's wrist to make sure they would know who was the first baby born.

The biggest problem was not giving the names to the boys but to find clothes for them, especially as they had so little money. Eventually, Grandpa and Grandma were helped by friends who gave little gifts of clothing for their twin sons. For twins, we were fairly large: Uncle Russell was six and a quarter pounds and Daddy was six pounds. We were actually Sabbath babies because we were born about nine o'clock Friday night. Of course, we did not go to church that day, and neither did Grandma, but Grandpa was able to go and surprise the members of Hamilton church with the news that Grandma had given birth to identical twin sons. This caused quite an excitement in the church, and many people were very anxious to see these new additions to the church. The next Sabbath, Grandma and Grandpa carried us to church, and of course we became the great center of attraction. Grandma was especially proud of her baby boys.

Uncle Russell and Daddy remember some teenage girls taking turns caring for us in Sabbath school and church. Years later, a number of the women told us how they loved to hold us in church. From that first time in Sabbath school and church, we have not missed church more than a few times. Almost every time it was when we were sick or in hospital.

We were very active little infants, and our crying really upset Great-grandpa Bailey and this caused some difficulties for Grandma and Grandpa—so much so that quite a few nights Grandma had to take us out into the laundry at the back of the house and close all the doors in the hope that Great-grandpa could not hear us crying. Of course, because there were two, when one woke up crying he often woke up the other one, and there was a duet of crying.

Grandma never stopped loving her two little boys, but maybe because of the surprise of having two children at once and the poverty of the home, our parents did not have another child for fourteen and a half years. Then our sister, Delma Alice, (her second name after Great-grandma Bailey) was born, and more than three and a half years later our young brother Lynden John (John after Great-grandpa Bailey) was born. From the earliest time Grandma Standish had great hopes that her two boys would become workers for Jesus.

> And she vowed a vow, and said, O LORD of hosts, if thou wilt indeed look on the affliction of thine handmaid, and remember me, and not forget thine handmaid, but wilt give unto thine handmaid a man child, then I will give him unto the LORD all the days of his life. . . .
> 1 Samuel 1:11

Chapter 7

Baby Shows

We have no memory of our first 2 years of life; however, Grandma, not uncommonly, spoke to us about our early life. During this time Grandpa had almost no income. He was on what was called the "dole," meaning that he got a limited help from the government. Also, every week Grandpa would work one or two days in a gravel pit using a pick and shovel to break up the gravel and load it onto trucks.

Until we were sixteen years of age and went to college, Grandma always insisted on dressing us alike, which did not help people tell us apart. However, as mothers somehow do, she could recognize almost immediately which one was Uncle Russell and which one was Daddy. Grandpa also learned, but not as fast as Grandma.

It was probably slightly easier to tell us apart than some identical twins because (as it was to be discovered as we grew older) we were mirror-image twins. They are twins in which one is left-handed and one is right-handed, so that the right side of the face of one corresponds to the left side of the face of the other, and of course the reverse was true. So, though we do not think much about it, all of us have slight differences between the two sides of our faces. You may not have thought about that, and even if you look at people you may not be able to see any significant differences.

Later, a little mole appeared on the side of Uncle Russell's head, and many people looked for that mole to decide which one was Uncle Russell and which one was Daddy. But often those who could not make a quick identification of us would just simply call each one of us "twin." In that way they could not make a mistake. However, even to this time in our lives, we still have many people calling us by the name of our brother. We are so used to it, we usually do not even try to correct them.

Grandma was very proud of her twins, and she knew that "they were the finest twins in all the city of Newcastle," at that time a city of 250,000 people. These were poor times, but it was also a time when it was fashionable to have many baby contests. There was a small entry fee, and parents could enter their children in different categories. Grandma decided to enter Uncle Russell and Daddy in the twin contest. Of course, being twins, there were not many entries. We remember Grandma saying that the most there ever was in the contest were seven sets of twins. Great-auntie Vera also encouraged Grandma to enter her boys in this contest, and Great-auntie Vera would travel with Grandma to these contests. (Great-auntie Vera was very much older than Grandma. She was the third child in the family, and Grandma was the last of eleven children.)

At the first contest they attended, of course Grandma and Great-auntie Vera were seriously looking at the other twins, and they were confident that their boys would be chosen. Grandma had done everything to fix us up and make us look our very best in our little short-pants suits. So it was indeed, we won that contest and every contest in which we were entered, although the number of entries decreased, we believe, to as low as four. Other mothers probably expected that the judges were not going to chose their twins; however, on one occasion, twins of another family were announced as the winners instead of the Standish twins. So certain were Grandma and Great-auntie Vera that the judges had announced the wrong name, that Great-auntie Vera went to them and told them they had announced the wrong name. Sure enough, to the disappointment of the other family and the embarrassment of the judges, the judges had to announce that they had made a mistake and that the winners were the Standish twins.

However, there was one twin contest which we did not win. It was a contest for the twins who looked most alike. Maybe the judges wanted to stimulate more interest in the twin category because there were so few entries. Of course, paternal twins (twins who could be boy and boy, girl and girl, or even boy and girl who may not look any more alike than normal brothers and sisters in the family) obviously could not enter for the contest in that category. Therefore, there were not many entries from the much more uncommon identical twins, and the judges decided that the Williams twins were the most alike. These were girls very close to our own age. Mother was to wonder whether the reason we did not look quite as much alike was because we were mirror image twins.

There was an interesting sequel to this. In 1951, when both sets of twins were seventeen years old, Mrs. Williams and her four children were converted into the Seventh-day Adventist Church at the crusade held in Newcastle by the powerful New Zealand evangelist, Pastor George Burnside. They became members of the very church we attended, and of course we got to know them well. They had an older sister and a younger brother. Sadly, one of the Williams twins died relatively young from cancer. Also, while barely in his 60s, their younger brother died of a heart attack.

So proud had Grandma become of her boys that she decided that she should enter one of them in the single baby contest. Of course, this contest had many more entries. She chose Uncle Russell because he was a little heavier than Daddy, and she believed that would be favorable to the decision of the judges. But this proved that her own evaluation of her sons was exaggerated, for Uncle Russell did not win that contest.

As you know, Uncle Russell and Daddy have perfectly straight hair. When we were young, at least until we were about six months of age, we had little hair. But once our hair started to grow, Grandma would often curl our hair. We were too young to protest; however, we have one photograph from when we were two years of age to remind us of this effort to improve our appearance.

There was another feature of which Grandma was delighted. She was the first mother ever in the city of Newcastle to purchase a twin stroller for her boys. It was purchased at a store owned by a Jew named Mr. Samuels. Later, when as nine-year-olds we went to live with Great-grandpa Bailey after the death of Great-grandma Bailey, we got to know Mr. Samuels. He was then an old man, very similar in age to Great-grandpa Bailey, and he lived three doors from us. Actually, there were three men, including Great-grandpa Bailey, who had a strange contest to see which one would live the longest. Great-grandpa seemed very pleased when he outlived the other two men before his death at age 83.

Now we realize that contests such as these baby contests are not God's way of doing things. God does not judge us by outward appearance, but by the heart.

> But the Lord said unto Samuel, Look not on his countenance, or on the height of his stature; because I have refused him: for the Lord seeth not as man seeth; for man looketh on the outward appearance, but the Lord looketh on the heart. 1 Samuel 16:7

Even though Grandma so loved her boys, she never indulged us and was very firm in our work and chores. We are so thankful for such a mother, because we were not easy children to manage, and we gave her not a little heartache. Every mother who is firm but loving will have a rich heritage with her children.

> Her children arise up, and call her blessed; her husband also, and he praiseth her. Proverbs 31:28

Chapter 8

Early Life

When Uncle Russell and Daddy were very little boys they lived with your Great-grandpa and Great-grandma Bailey. Great-grandfather Bailey was born in 1865 in Newcastle, Australia. When he was fifteen he began working in a coal mine in the Newcastle area where he worked for 25 years. He then became a cleaner of steamtrain engines for another 25 years before he retired at 65 years of age. In those days the work week at first was 48 hours and later 44 hours per week.

Great-grandma Bailey was born in Newcastle, England, in 1871. When she was nine years of age, she came with her parents by boat to Newcastle, Australia. Her father, your maternal Great-grandfather, was a Scotsman by the name of Mr. Craig, and your maternal Great-grandmother was English. On the boat out to Australia, when the boat was near South Africa, somehow Great-grandma fell overboard into the ocean and a brave young sailor jumped into the ocean after her and held her up in the ocean until they both could be rescued. That was in 1880, when Great-grandma was only nine years old.

If Great-grandma had not been rescued, Uncle Russell and Daddy would never have been born. Great-grandma's family chose to live in Newcastle, Australia, called after Newcastle, England, where Great-grandma was born. Both cities were built near very rich coal mines and developed big steel mills where iron ore is smelted in very hot furnaces to make steel.

Always, these steel mills are built where there is much coal because it takes two tons of coal to smelt one ton of iron ore. Therefore, it is cheaper to transport the iron ore from the mine to the coal than for the coal to be transported to the iron ore deposits.

Great-grandma married Great-grandpa Bailey in 1886, when he was twenty years old and she was only fifteen years of age. They would have eleven children. They had six daughters and five sons. The second child died when she was very young—about two years old—when her dress was set on fire by a little boy who lived next door. One of the other daughters died during infancy when somehow she was accidentally strangled by a young helper.

Two of the boys had tragic experiences. About 1922 the youngest boy, Great-uncle Fred, then sixteen, disappeared from home and was never seen again by his family. Grandma, the youngest child, was then about ten years old. Great-grandma Bailey did everything to try to find Great-uncle Fred, but she never did. She even traveled down to Sydney when she saw a photo of a ship's crew in the newspaper and thought one of the sailors looked like Great-uncle Fred. The captain lined up all his sailors for a full roll call, but there was no sign of Great-uncle Fred. Fred had been born in 1906.

An older brother, Great-uncle Cecil, was born in 1900 and at the age of 33 was working as a tram-conductor. On a wet day he slipped off the outside running board of the tram and died in the hospital from his injuries, as I explained earlier. Thus only seven of the eleven children died from natural causes.

Grandma Standish was the youngest child, born in 1912. The other six children were Great-auntie Amy, the first-born; Great-auntie Vera, the third-born; Great-uncle Oliver, the fourth-born; Great-uncle Clarence, the fifth-born; Great-uncle Jim, the sixth-born; and Great-auntie Alice the ninth-born. Great-auntie Alice lived the longest of any of the children to 86 years of age. Grandma Standish lived the shortest life of those who survived to die naturally at the age of 61.

After Grandmother came home with her newly born twin sons, Uncle Russell and Daddy lived with our great-grandparents. Because Great-grandfather Bailey was not a converted man, our crying really irritated him. However, we were to live with Grandpa and Grandma Bailey for eighteen months before Grandma and Grandpa decided it was only sensible for the family to leave and find new accommodations. The tension in the home was the reason for leaving our Great-grandparents home; however, it was a most difficult time. It was still in the depth of the depression of the 1930s, and Grandpa had no regular work. A large number of people were not employed because of the economic difficulties of the Great Depression from 1929 through the 1930s.

Grandma has told us that it was common for her to stand in lines sometimes a half-mile long to receive the handouts—usually bread and milk—from the government which were given to the poor people of Newcastle. However, somehow they survived and Grandma was able to feed her two boys well. Of course, Uncle Russell and Daddy do not remember this part of our lives. However, we did learn that we began to walk at thirteen months old. Maybe we were just a little later than average because we had been born about three weeks prematurely.

At fifteen months old, Daddy had a very painful experience. At this time Grandma and Grandpa were sitting in the backyard of our Great-grandparents' home at 78 Dumaresq Street in the suburb of Hamilton in Newcastle. Somehow Uncle Russell and Daddy were at the back of the house and started to toddle down to Grandpa and Grandma. We do not know whether either of them saw us coming. Unfortunately, between the back of the house and where Grandpa and Grandma were sitting, reading the paper, there was a smoldering rubbish heap. As we toddled down, Daddy's path took him right to the smoldering heap. He tripped on the heap, fell over, and was seriously burned on his right foot and abdomen. Very alarmed, Grandpa rushed to the public telephone and called an ambulance, which took Daddy to the Royal Newcastle Hospital. Daddy was in the hospital for five weeks. They must have been five long weeks for a little infant. Uncle Russell used to wonder where Daddy was. In those days little children were not allowed to go into a hospital. Of course, Grandpa and Grandma visited Daddy, and I would always cry when they were leaving me.

The incident left me with permanent burn marks on my right foot and on the middle of my abdomen. Grandma wondered whether the scar on my abdomen was caused by the fire or whether it was caused by using some of the skin on Daddy's abdomen to graft onto the foot.

However, Daddy is more inclined to believe both were caused by the fire because, at that time the skill of grafting was not nearly as well developed as it is today. Grandma told me that when Daddy came back home, now sixteen months of age, I had forgotten how to walk and had to learn to walk all over again. Sometimes burns can become infected and cause other problems and, in some rare cases, result in death. How Daddy thanks God that He protected me and spared my life! There is no doubt that Jesus cares for children.

> But Jesus said, Suffer little children, and forbid them not, to come unto me: for of such is the kingdom of heaven. Matthew 19:14

Chapter 9

Living in a Bag Shack

From the age of eighteen months to nearly three years of age, Uncle Russell and Daddy, along with their parents, lived in a bag shack. You will find this hard to believe, but in the great depression quite a few people were forced to live in such conditions in Australia. Once again neither Uncle Russell nor Daddy remembers living in this bag shack. It was located in the Newcastle suburb of Charlestown, which is a few miles farther away from Newcastle city than Hamilton. Grandpa and Grandma felt that they had to move because Great-grandpa Bailey was so hard to live with. He was constantly angry about the crying of Uncle Russell and Daddy, and he often upset Grandma who did not know what to do to make him happy.

The bag shack which Grandpa and Grandma had purchased in Charlestown cost them ten pounds (20 dollars). When we left, Grandpa and Grandma donated the bag shack to the Rose family, a Seventh-day Adventist family which was even poorer than we were. Uncle Russell and Daddy remember them well because later, when at nine years old we attended the Hamilton church, they attended there also. Their oldest child Ron was just a little younger than Uncle Russell and Daddy.

Uncle Russell and Daddy know very little about what life was like living in the bag shack, although there were other similar shacks in the same area. One incident which Grandma related to us was concerning another little boy older than us who pulled Daddy's souwester off his head. A souwester was a little hat which covered both the head and the back of the neck. When this little boy threw Daddy's souwester into a mud puddle, Daddy's cry led Grandma to discover the situation.

After living in the bag shack for perhaps a year and a half, our parents moved to Blackalls, not too far from Toronto and almost twenty miles from Newcastle. There we stayed with a Seventh-day Adventist family for a few months.

It was when we were three years old that Grandpa was able to find his first permanent employment as a fettler (one who is part of a team to help keep the railroad tracks in good repair) for the New South Wales government railway system. Even though the salary was only about three pounds ten shillings a week ($7.00), it provided, in the very weak economy of Australia at that time, the first secure regular income for the family. This led to a move to our first rental home in Boolaroo, about twelve miles southwest of Newcastle. We first lived on Seventh Street. This is the first home which Uncle Russell and Daddy can remember. Therefore this is the first place where our recollections begin. Later we lived on Fifth Street.

We may have lived in a bag shack on this earth, but if faithful to Jesus, we will live in mansions in heaven, and Daddy prays that you, too, will be always faithful to Jesus and therefore live in heavenly mansions.

> Let not your heart be troubled: ye believe in God, believe also in me. In my Father's house are many mansions: if it were not so, I would have told you. I go to prepare a place for you. And if I go and prepare a place for you, I will come again, and receive you unto myself; that where I am, there ye may be also. John 14:1–3

Chapter 10

Attending Boolaroo Seventh-day Adventist Church

There was only once that Uncle Russell and Daddy remember Great-grandfather Bailey coming to visit us when we lived at Boolaroo, and he stayed with us for a couple of days. He had brought out with him his scissors and his haircut clippers. As far as we know, electric clippers were either not available then, so these were all hand clippers. Grandma thought it was wonderful that Great-grandpa could cut our hair, for it would save her six-pence (five cents) each for the hair-cut of her boys. Daddy was the first chosen to receive the hair-cut. Great-grandpa Bailey took Daddy out into the yard and there he cut Daddy's hair. He cut, and he cut, and he cut until he had cut all the hair off Daddy's head! When Grandma saw it she was horrified, and she asked Great-grandpa what he had done. He said he had tried to stop, but it was uneven and eventually he thought the best thing was to cut the whole hair off Daddy's head. Grandma refused to allow Great-grandpa to cut Uncle Russell's hair, and so for many weeks it was very easy for people to tell the difference between Uncle Russell and Daddy. Of course Daddy was embarrassed when people commented on his lack of hair. But hair grows, and it grew again back to its normal length.

From the age of three until just after we had turned nine years old, Uncle Russell and Daddy attended the little wooden Seventh-day Adventist church at Boolaroo. It was located on the side of a gentle slope not far from where we lived. Even when we moved from Seventh Street to Fifth Street, though that was farther away, we still had a short walk to church. This was very important to Grandma and Grandpa, for we had no vehicles whatsoever—not even a bicycle.

When we were young, some of the older children in the church would ask to take care of us during the church service. This was especially true of Evelyn Harrington. Evelyn was probably about nine or ten years of age when we were four. While it may not have been the best thing to do, she would draw us little pictures to occupy our attention and keep us from getting into mischief.

Many little incidents come back to Daddy's memory of that church. He remembers how Grandma used to teach us our doctrinal text, and every day she would rehearse us until we knew it well enough that we could recite it at the Missionary Volunteer meeting Sabbath afternoon. Once a quarter we would take the doctrinal texts exam. At that time, it was much simpler for little children than for older children and adults. Because we could not write, Grandma would read us the questions, and we would tell her the answers. Sometimes she would prompt us a little, and we would complete the doctrinal text exam. Uncle Russell and Daddy were excited when the exams would come back marked from the conference office accompanied by a little certificate stating that we had passed the doctrinal texts examination.

We well remember one occasion when a minister came to the church to preach on temperance. In the afternoon, at the Missionary Volunteer meeting, the minister made an appeal for everyone to sign the temperance pledge never to smoke or to drink alcohol. Though we were young at the time, maybe five or six, Uncle Russell and Daddy signed that pledge. We did not fully understand the implications of signing the pledge, but we believe that that was a very important signature which was placed on that paper, for we have never forgotten that we signed that pledge. What a wonderful thing it is for all children to sign the temperance pledge and to be faithful to it for the rest of their lives!

Uncle Russell and Daddy cannot forget the happy times we had in Sabbath school. There was a small room under the back of the church where the children's Sabbath school was conducted. There were times when Uncle Russell and Daddy were the only children in that Sabbath school. We look back and wonder at the special efforts which the teacher, Sister Lillian Paynter, painstakingly took so that we would have a carefully planned Sabbath school. Oh, it was very simple. She would teach us a little Christian song, and she always prepared the sand tray to illustrate the Bible story which we had studied for that week. Mrs. Paynter used a picture roll, as so many teachers did. This picture illustrated a major aspect of the story which we were studying. Many of the recollections we have today of Bible stories were no doubt forged in that little Sabbath school.

However, there were times when there were other children. We remember when the Ling family came to Boolaroo church. At that time Mr. Ling was not a Seventh-day Adventist, but he was baptized later into the Seventh-day Adventist faith after they had moved away to Morpeth, about twenty or so miles north of Newcastle. At the time the Ling's came to Boolaroo church they had two children—Doug, who was older than Uncle Russell and Daddy, and Cynthia, who was younger than us. In later years Doug Ling was to become our closest friend at high school. Sadly, our friend Doug left the Seventh-day Adventist faith, and Uncle Russell and Daddy did not hear from him for many years, although in my early years in Sydney, Daddy had spent much time with Doug and his New Zealand wife, who was a very fine Christian. However, Doug, who trained as a nurse at the Sydney Adventist Hospital where he met his first wife, became unfaithful to his wife, and they were divorced. He died at the age of 56.

What a privilege Daddy had less than one year before Doug died to discover where he lived and to meet with him again! He was now married to another woman—not a Seventh-day Adventist—and they had a young daughter. Daddy spoke to him very earnestly about spiritual matters, and he seemed to respond well. Daddy told Uncle Russell, and Uncle Russell telephoned him a few months later when he returned to Australia from mission service in Southeast Asia. Uncle Russell had a lovely spiritual talk with him and arranged to meet with him, but that was never to take place, for less than two weeks later he died of a heart attack. It was Uncle Russell's sad privilege to conduct our friend Doug's funeral. We both pray that he had settled his life with Jesus at that time.

Doug's sister Cynthia is now Mrs. Bill Turner. Of course, you have met them on your visits back to the Newcastle area of Australia.

There were some sad experiences while we were at Boolaroo church. I think of the Bowen family. It was so sad when their family left to live elsewhere. However, one of their sons, Jack Bowen, who was much older than Uncle Russell and Daddy, met with us from time to time when we spoke at meetings held near his home in Foster. He was then a strong leader for God.

There was another family which fascinated us, the Marshman family. They were very careful health reformers and yet seemed a little strange in some ways. Maybe we thought so because Grandpa and Grandma were not, at that point, as strict as the Marshmans were in health reform. They were very sincere people. Later Mrs. Marshman was to write health messages and provide healthy recipes for the *Australasian* (now *South Pacific) Record.*

Our parents had made strong headway in health reform, and when we were three years of age they had decided to put flesh out of their diet. (Not that they ate much meat; it was too expensive on the little money that they had.) From that point on, our parents raised us on an ovo-lacto vegetarian diet.

There were other people we remember who unfortunately did not have their husbands in the truth—Mrs. Black, and Mrs. Blue. There was old Mrs. Stenton and her daughter, Mrs. Thompson, whose husband was not a Seventh-day Adventist and who worked as an official in a coal mine. He always seemed to Uncle Russell and Daddy to be a very conservative man, but, though he was not unpleasant, we did not feel very comfortable with him. The wonderful sequel is that later he did become a Seventh-day Adventist and lived to well be over 90 years before passing to his rest in the hope of the return of Jesus.

There was Jack Ladd. He came from a farming family in the Warner's Bay area near Lake Macquarie, not too far from Boolaroo where the church was situated. What a faithful younger man he was, even though he was of relatively low intelligence. However, he served as a deacon in the church.

The saddest experience which happened in the Boolaroo church happened when Uncle Russell and Daddy were about six years of age.

We had so admired Mr. Harrigan. He worked in a coal mine. He was a strong, straight-back, dignified man. He was the elder of the church. The most enduring memory which we have of Mr. Harrigan is that when he was singing hymns on the platform, he would tap his foot to the meter of the music. He had been a Seventh-day Adventist for more than twenty years with his family, but eventually his oldest son got into some trouble with the law. This devastated and humiliated Mr. Harrigan, and to our great shock, Mr. Harrigan and the family left the Seventh-day Adventist Church. Even as little boys we knew that that was a very sad thing, and how we missed those two children, Evelyn and Neville, who by this time were perhaps ten and twelve years old respectively. They had an older sister, Marjorie, who had grown up before her family left the church. We do not remember meeting her then, but now she is in her late 80s and lives just a couple of doors away from Grandma Basham. She became Mrs. Tad Fisher, but her husband died quite a few years ago.

When Mr. Harrigan left the Boolaroo church, very soon thereafter, Grandpa was ordained to be the elder. He was still a very young man of 27, but there was no one else in the church who was suited to that responsibility. That began a period of 58 years before Grandpa's death that almost continuously he was an elder successively of the Hamilton church in Newcastle, the Lismore church in Northern New South Wales, the Morpeth Vale, in Adelaide, South Australia, the Auburn church in Melbourne, the Croydon church in Melbourne, the Euroa church in rural Victoria, and finally the Ararat church near the center of the state of Victoria. Grandpa always sought faithfully to live up to God's qualification for an elder.

> This is a true saying, If a man desire the office of a bishop, he desireth a good work. A bishop then must be blameless, the husband of one wife, vigilant, sober, of good behaviour, given to hospitality, apt to teach; not given to wine, no striker, not greedy of filthy lucre; but patient, not a brawler, not covetous; one that ruleth well his own house, having his children in subjection with all gravity; (for if a man know not how to rule his own

house, how shall he take care of the church of God?) not a novice, lest being lifted up with pride he fall into the condemnation of the devil. Moreover he must have a good report of them which are without; lest he fall into reproach and the snare of the devil. 1 Timothy 3:1–7

Chapter 11

Two Scared Boys

When Uncle Russell and Daddy were little boys living in Boolaroo, they saw Grandpa only on the weekends because he had to often work on the railroad tracks at long distances away from Boolaroo. On Monday mornings he would walk about one mile to the Cockle Creek railway station and travel to the closest station where he would be working that week. He worked on the main north-south railway line, usually south of Newcastle and as far south as the Hawksberry River Bridge about 30 miles north of Sydney.

On one occasion, Grandpa and his team were working in the one-mile-long Woy Woy Tunnel, the longest train tunnel in Australia. As fettlers (repairmen of the rail) they had to know the schedule when the trains were coming from the north and from the south. Because it was a main railway line between Sydney and Brisbane, there were many trains each day. Besides passenger trains, there were trains carrying merchandise, coal, cattle and sheep back and forth from country and city locations. However, one particular train caught them by surprise. Grandpa and his fellow workers were trapped in the tunnel with no way to escape, when they heard the thunderous roar of the train coming. They had been riding their man-powered trolley on the tracks, which was the common method of travel for fettlers. All they could do was jump off the trolley, run as far as they could, and drop down as close to the wall of the tunnel and away from the tracks. Thanks to the protection of the Lord, no one was harmed when the train raced through, although the trolley was smashed to pieces.

During the week, all the fettlers lived in little tents provided by the New South Wales Government Railway. These tents were not very comfortable, and they were especially cold in the winter and even worse any time there was heavy rain. When Grandpa was 25 years of age, he suffered serious pain in his body. He had to miss five weeks of work altogether, during which time he was diagnosed at the Sydney Seventh-day Adventist Sanitarium at Wahroonga (now the Sydney Adventist Hospital) with rheumatoid arthritis. Uncle Russell now believes that he had ankylosing spondilitis, a condition which Uncle Russell has and cousin James has. It is a hereditary condition that can be life-threatening if severe enough, and it brings great pain especially in the neck and shoulder areas and makes mobility very difficult. However, it is environmentally triggered. Somehow, in spite of Daddy being an identical twin with Uncle Russell, he never did develop ankylosing spondilitis, and therefore he has not had to suffer the way Grandpa, Uncle Russell, or James have suffered. From time to time through the rest of his life, Grandpa had significant pain, and it would be very difficult to move his head. He began to refer to it as the "screws." Whenever Grandpa would say, "The screws are bad this morning," we knew that he had much pain. Grandpa worked for the New South Wales Government Railway until 1943 when he was 31 years of age.

Every year the railway workers had a picnic day for themselves and their families. One year the picnic was at Spear's Point, in walking distance from where we lived in Boolaroo, so the whole family went to the picnic grounds. They had races for children of every age as well as for the railway workers and another race for the railway workers' wives. Only one event do I remember well. I believe Uncle Russell and Daddy were about four years old at the time, and we were lined up with all the other boys of the same age. The starter explained to us that we could not start running until he had said, "Ready, set, go!" Then we were told to run as fast as we could. We do not know how long the race was, but it was probably 50 yards. As soon as the starter said, "Go!" Uncle Russell and Daddy ran as fast as they could run. Daddy was leading all the other boys. Then Grandma very excitedly called out, "Come on, Colin, Come on Colin!" Daddy stopped running and started walking over to

Grandma. She was devastated because she wanted her little boy to win. Even Uncle Russell slowed down. We often wished that we had always been as obedient to Mother's commands in other aspects of our lives. However, Grandma made amends to the family "honor" by winning the railway workers' wives' race.

It was while living in Boolaroo that Daddy remembers first showing an interest in reading. Daddy was about four years of age at the time, and he remembers it well. Grandpa was reading the newspaper, and Daddy hopped on Grandpa's knee and started to look at the newspaper Grandpa was reading. Grandpa kept reading, and somehow Daddy was fascinated, and he soon started asking Grandpa, "What is this word?" "What is that word?" Each time Grandpa would tell him what the words were.

Also, during this time, Grandpa and Grandma had befriended a very downtrodden family, hoping they could help them find the Seventh-day Adventist faith. They were especially burdened for the mother. She had quite a number of children, and she was very poor because her husband was a heavy alcohol drinker and earned very little money. On one occasion when she was expecting another child, the little girl of about three years of age came to live with us for several weeks. Grandma and Grandpa decided to care for her until this lady was well enough to care for her again. Both Grandma and Grandpa learned to love this little girl, and she seemed to be very happy at our home. Eventually the time came when the mother came to take her back to her home. The poor little girl cried. She did not want to leave our home because she probably remembered that her own home was not a happy home. We often wonder what happened to that little girl who lived in such a poor home environment. How thankful Uncle Russell and Daddy were for a Christian home!

Early in our lives Uncle Russell and Daddy had a great fear of heights. Why we had this great fear we do not know, but have it we did. We hated to cross railroad tracks because we were afraid of the height, of the pedestrian bridge over the tracks. We did not like being in elevators because they took us high above the ground.

On one occasion Grandpa was walking Uncle Russell and Daddy from Boolaroo across to Teralba. That is where the family lived whose little girl stayed with us for a number of weeks when she was three years old. Grandma was already there. It was summer time, and we were both dressed up in little white suits with white tops and white short pants. Everything went well until we came to a little bridge which crossed Cockle Creek. Uncle Russell and Daddy were afraid to go over the bridge even though it was not very high. We did *not* want to go over the bridge, so we both broke loose from Grandpa. It had rained apparently not long before we were there, and there were a number of mud puddles. As Grandpa tried to catch us, Daddy slipped over in one of these puddles and, of course, he got mud all over his little white suit. Grandpa was very upset, and he immediately chased him and caught him, and Daddy received quite a beating from Grandpa. He then demanded Uncle Russell to come to him at once, and he took us by the hand. With both of us resisting he dragged us over the bridge while we both closed our eyes so we could not see the water below us. When we reached the house where the people lived, Grandma was also upset to see one of her boys in such a mess. As you can imagine, they were not easy days for us.

All children and young people must learn never to do dangerous things just for a thrill, for we must do all that we can to protect the life that God had given to us. However, there is no need to fear when we wholly surrender to God's will.

> Thou shalt not be afraid for the terror by night; nor for the arrow that flieth by day; Nor for the pestilence that walketh in darkness; nor for the destruction that wasteth at noonday. A thousand shall fall at thy side, and ten thousand at thy right hand; but it shall not come nigh thee. Psalm 91:5–7

> There is no fear in love; but perfect love casteth out fear. . . . 1 John 4:18

> For God hath not given us the spirit of fear; but of power, and of love, and of a sound mind. 2 Timothy 1:7

Chapter 12

Personal Scary Moments

When Uncle Russell and Daddy were little boys, they soon developed many fears. In the last story I told that Grandpa was not home except on weekends; therefore, we did not get to know Grandpa as well as children should get to know their father. Most of our time was spent with Grandma.

One night when Uncle Russell and Daddy were about four years old, Grandma decided she would play a "game" with us—or what she thought was a game. She told us that she was going to run away from us, and she ran and hid behind a door. We were not even dressed except for a little top; however, we began to cry as we ran out of the house and down the hill from the little home in which we lived, running as fast as we could toward the main street, hoping that we could find Grandma. It was some time before Grandma realized what had happened and we were no where to be seen. Quickly She came running to find her two little boys, down the hill and toward the main road. Eventually she caught up with us as we passed the Anglican church on the left hand side of the street. We were so happy to see Grandma again, and you can be sure that she never played that kind of a trick on us again.

On another occasion when we were about four years old, Uncle Russell and Daddy had wandered down our street to the corner with the main street. There was a butcher's shop on that corner. Perhaps it was out of curiosity that we went into the butcher's shop, but when the young assistant butcher saw us, he decided to play a prank on us. He grabbed both of us and dragged us to the cooler where all the animal carcasses were hanging down by hooks. Then he told us he was going to put us in the cooler and make mincemeat out of us to sell to the customers. Of course, we were terrified, and when he put us in the cooler and closed the door, it was black as midnight when the moon and stars are not shining. Both of us started to scream, for we really thought he meant what he had said. Imagine how relieved we were when the door opened! He was laughing loudly, for he thought it was a great joke, but it was not funny to us. We ran back home as fast as we could up the hill, and I do not have to tell you that we never went into that butcher's shop again.

Another time when we were about the same age, Uncle Russell and Daddy were down on the other side of the main road right outside the Boolaroo post office when along came three children somewhat older than us. They had with them a number of firecrackers, and they thought they would have some fun with us. These firecrackers were not the usual kind, but a very cheap kind that exploded when they were thrown down on the ground. We called them "throw-me-downs." Of course, coming from a poor family, we had not seen throw-me-downs, and when the children saw us they decided to scare us. Coming close to us, they threw down a cracker with a BANG, which really scared Uncle Russell and Daddy! Then they threw another one behind us, and we thought we would never get away from these bigger boys. To our relief, they did not have very many of these throw-me-downs, and soon we were able to run back home.

Eventually, the owners of our first home on Seventh Street needed the home for themselves, and Grandpa and Grandma moved into a home on Fifth Street, Boolaroo. This was a big and difficult decision for our parents, for they were paying five shillings (50 cents) a week for the home in Seventh Street, and now they had to pay seven shillings and sixpence a week (75 cents), a 50 percent increase. They wondered if they could manage that amount and still live on the small salary which Grandpa was earning as a fettler on the New South Wales Government Railway. God was good and we always had food and some clothing and a roof over our heads. God promises to care for His children.

> I have been young, and now am old; yet have I not seen the righteous forsaken, nor his seed begging bread.
> Psalm 37:25

Chapter 13

Expelled from School

When Uncle Russell and Daddy were just four and one-half years old Grandma decided that she would send us to the Boolaroo public school. We remember her taking us there. It was a new and strange experience being with a large number of other children. We forget now how many children were there. It probably was not much more than one hundred or a hundred and fifty, but that was a large number to little boys who had rarely played with other children.

We remember the most common activities of the children when the classes were in recess. The children would jostle for a place at the water fountains where they would make suds from little pieces of soap they had brought from home. Uncle Russell and Daddy wanted to get some soap so we could make suds, too. We forget now whether Grandma gave us a little piece of soap or whether we just took it, but we were so happy to be able to be able to make soap suds like the other children were doing.

I can remember, too, that often we sat on the floor in circles in our little kindergarten class as the teacher taught or read to us. However, at four and one-half, obviously we were not easy to manage and not ready for school. One day the teacher gave us a note asking us to be very careful with it and make sure that when we arrived home to give it to Grandma. Little did we know what was written in that note. When we arrived home, we faithfully gave the letter to Grandma. She read it and said that the teacher believed we were too young to be in school and that we should be withdrawn from school until we turned five years of age. Both Uncle Russell and Daddy cried. We felt so ashamed that we had been put out of school. Uncle Russell and Daddy turned five October 27, 1938. Grandma did not take us back to school immediately. She waited for the new school year to start late January 1939, when we were five years and three months old.

We cannot forget the day we were taken back to school. Neither of us wanted to go back to school, because we had been "expelled." Grandma had to take us by her hands, and she had to almost drag us to the school. We were even more uncooperative after we crossed the main road, for each of us tried to hang on to the small gate post at the school entrance. Grandma persisted, and we were taken into the school grounds and reenrolled in the Boolaroo Public Primary (Elementary) School. However, we soon settled down, and no one seemed to say anything about our being put out of the school the year before.

Another little incident happened while we were living in the house on Fifth Street. To make a few shillings extra per week, Grandma helped clean the house of Mrs. Stewart, who lived just a few houses down the hill from where we lived. With a name like that, her husband had to have come from Scottish forebears. One day Uncle Russell and Daddy found a little box of matches, and when we opened it there were a few new matches in the box. What a delight this was to five year olds! We found pieces of paper in the gutter, and we set them alight, altogether unaware of the danger of fire. A lady saw us and told us to stop, which we did. We then ran up to Mrs. Stewart's house where Grandma was working at the time. We crawled under Mrs. Stewart's house and began to light a fire, thinking that no one would find us there. It was not a big fire, and it did not reach up to the floorboards of the house; however, Mrs. Stewart probably smelled smoke coming up through the floorboards. Whatever it was, she came down and saw Uncle Russell and Daddy playing with fire under her house. She immediately commanded us to put out the fire, which we did. But very quickly she had informed Grandma of what her boys were up to, and Grandma was absolutely devastated to see her little boys doing something that could have proven to be so dangerous. Once again, God was good to us in that we did no damage, and we never again remember playing with matches. Grandmother took care that we would not forget the wrong thing which we had done, for her consequences were very painful to us.

Chapter 14

We Move to Cardiff

The year 1939 was a very significant year in the world, for the Second World War began in September of that year. It was also a very significant year in the Standish family. Once again we had to move because the owners of the home which we rented on Fifth Street was needed for one of their family members. Grandma searched far and wide but could find no suitable home in Boolaroo. Eventually she found a home in Cardiff, several miles closer to Newcastle, where her parents still lived in the suburb of Hamilton. This home created a great challenge for our parents because instead of rent for seven shillings and sixpence (75 cents) a week, they had to pay thirteen shillings and sixpence (one dollar and 35 cents) a week in rent. By this time Grandpa's salary was a little more than four pound a week (eight dollars); however, Uncle Russell and Daddy were growing up quickly, and the cost of supporting them was increasing. The house was not special in any way; it had but four rooms and a back veranda. It had a large kitchen with a coal-burning stove on which Grandma cooked the food. It had a very small lounge room straight off the kitchen, and behind the kitchen and the lounge room were two bedrooms, one for Grandpa and Grandma and the other for Uncle Russell and Daddy.

The home was right by the main tracks for the Brisbane-Newcastle-Sydney Railway lines. Grandpa and Grandma were very afraid that their five-and-one-half-year-old boys might venture onto the tracks, and Grandma gave Uncle Russell and Daddy very strict instructions that we were forbidden ever to go onto the tracks. To the best of our memory, we never did. However, that began our fascination with trains. The home was also very close to the Cardiff Railway Station. We would see many trains—express trains or all-station passenger trains as well as trains carrying merchandise, coal, cattle, and sheep—passing along those lines.

What excited us most was when the Inter-city Express, commonly called "the flyer," thundered past our house on its way to Sydney or from Sydney back to Newcastle. The intercity express ran in both directions three times a day. Every morning at 7:55 a.m., the train would roar past our home. Most mornings we would rush to the veranda to see it power past the Cardiff Station on its way to its destination in Sydney. We would be home from school in the late afternoon to see the third of the Newcastle to Sydney expresses speed past our home at 4:55 p.m. Of course, except when it was vacation time, we were at school when the mid-day inter-city express passed our home in the middle of the day.

However, our joy was complete when in about 1942 they introduced the new 38 steam class engine to replace the 36 class engine which had for so many years sped the inter-city express on its two-hour-eighteen-minutes journey 107 miles between Newcastle, the sixth largest city of Australia, and Sydney, the largest city of Australia.

The 38 class engines were painted a glistening green. They were the first bullet-nosed steam engines in Australia, and ultimately they proved to be the last introduced into Australian railways. After that, the diesel engine took over. Now, as you now know, all the passenger trains between Sydney and Newcastle are electric trains. The trains which travel farther north are powered by diesel engines.

In our childhood and youth we greatly enjoyed train travel. It was especially exciting when we traveled to Sydney Central Station, where we watched the trains coming and going, often to far distant places in the country or interstate. However, the thrill we had then does not compare to the thrill of inter-galaxy travel which will be the wonderful experience of God's faithful people which will begin with the return of our Savior.

> For the Lord himself shall descend from heaven with a shout, with the voice of the archangel, and with the

trump of God: and the dead in Christ shall rise first: then we which are alive and remain shall be caught up together with them in the clouds, to meet the Lord in the air: and so shall we ever be with the Lord. 1 Thessalonians 4:16, 17

Chapter 15

New School

In July of 1939, Uncle Russell and Daddy moved from Boolaroo to Cardiff with Grandpa and Grandma. Little did we know the dramatic changes which were to take place in the world two months later—changes that would alter the direction of the world forever. Uncle Russell and Daddy were little boys of five and one-half. We had no thought about what the word "war" meant. Yes, by this time we had heard about the First World War and even the Boer War in South Africa in which Australian solders had fought.

The year before, we had watched the Anzac Parade. As you know there is a public holiday on April 25 every year, which commemorates the courageous efforts of the Australian and the New Zealand Army Corps (Anzac) to battle against the Turkish army which was entrenched on the cliffs above the ocean of Gallipoli. Sadly, many thousands of Australian and New Zealand young men were slaughtered in that battle. Many of them did not even make it to the shore before they were gunned down by the Turkish artillery. Daddy still remembers the parade as it marched through Martin Place, Sydney. There standing with his slouched Australian army hat was little Billy Hughes, a Welshman who had been the Prime Minister of Australia during the First World War. Even then he was beginning to look old. Yet, he continued many more years to take the salute at every Anzac parade each year. When he became too old to stand, he would sit on a chair. Still today the seat remains where Billy Hughes once sat at every Anzac Parade. On it is placed Billy Hughes' soldier's hat.

Of course with the huge crowds watching the Parade, we could not see it except as we sat on Grandpa's shoulders. First one and then the other would be hoisted up by Grandpa. Among those who were marching, we could see not only soldiers from the First World War of 1914–1918, but there were also soldiers from the Boer War, the war in South Africa when the British fought against the Afrikaners, 1899–1902. Some of them were beginning to get old by 1938. Of course, all of those Boer War soldiers are now dead. Recently, the last Australian First World War veteran died.

Going to a new school was very difficult, for Uncle Russell and Daddy. However, the lady who was principal of the infant schools, which included the kindergarten, first grade and second grade, seemed to be impressed with Uncle Russell and Daddy. Well we remember her words to Grandma, "These boys look like bright boys. I think I will put them into first grade rather than keep them in kindergarten." So a little more than half way through the year we were thrown into the lower first grade class. In hindsight, we believe that was a mistake. We missed so much of the preparation in learning to read and to do simple math. We have had a lifetime struggle with spelling, and it took many years before we became adequate readers. This led Uncle Russell and Daddy to receive a mark of zero out of twenty for spelling in our primary final at the end of sixth grade.

We have some interesting memories of school. Every morning in the infant school, we would start assembly with prayer. Well Daddy remembers, to his great embarrassment, reporting that one of the other students had his eyes open during prayer. When Daddy reported this to the head mistress, she pointed out that my eyes had to be open, too.

Daddy also remembers that we seemed to sing all the British patriotic songs and hardly any Australian songs. We would sing "Rule Britannia," "There Will Always be an England," "From Suva to Vancouver, from the Rand to Mandaly, the Empire is marching towards the Day." Even the other songs we were taught were English songs, such as "Dear little birdie brown built a nest in the old oak tree." Of course, there are no oak trees which grow naturally in Australia. This had to be an English children's song exported to Australia. We had to wait until our middle teenage years before we learned, "Kookaburra sits in an old gum tree. Merry, merry king of the woods is he"—a truly Australian song.

Our teacher in grade 2B was Miss Hemming. Somehow she took a fancy to Uncle Russell and Daddy, probably because we were twins. She even took us by bus to her -home for our seventh birthday. We remember her teaching us how to put our knife and fork together on our plate when we finished our meal. However, there was one thing that Miss Hemming unwittingly did which greatly disadvantaged Daddy. She noticed that he was left-handed and believed that there were many future options which would not be open to him if he wrote left-handed. She sent a note home to Grandma explaining this, saying, for example, that Daddy could not be a school teacher because he could not give right-handed children an example in penmanship. Grandma, of course, believed what the teacher said. She had not been educated in school beyond part-way through the eighth grade and probably accepted everything a teacher said. There was also a girl in the class who was left-handed, so Miss Hemming made a challenge saying that the first one to change completely over to using the right hand would be rewarded with a toffee apple. That was too much of an incentive for Daddy. Of course, he won the apple on a stick, as we called it. What children will do for such small rewards! In this case, the reward was an unhealthy one.

This effort to make a change did not affect Daddy much when he was in second grade, for we were still using a pencil to write. However, the next year, when Uncle Russell and Daddy were promoted from 2B to 3A, we were now required to use pen and ink. In those days there were no ballpoint pens, and fountain pens were too expensive for us to have, so we used the very simple nib pens. Every child in the class had an inkwell, and the nib would be placed in the inkwell to gather the ink. It would then be wiped sufficiently, hopefully not to produce any ink blots on the paper on which we were working, and we would write two or three words until the ink ran out and we would start all over again, place the nib in the ink, wipe off some of the ink, and then write again. With the lack of right hand dexterity, Daddy often left blots on his work. The new teacher probably did not know that Daddy had recently been changed from the left to the right hand, and when those blots went on his work or when the work appeared poorly written, he would be kept in school during recess time to repeat his work. That was very discouraging to Daddy, and the third grade saw him drop back in his school work. However, Uncle Russell and Daddy both did well enough to be promoted to 4A where we had the same teacher as we had in 3A.

When Daddy was in 4A, he sometimes got into difficulty for bad behavior, and on one occasion he was sent to be with the class taught by Mr. Petterfield, the principal. Daddy was amazed at how difficult the sixth class work was, and he was very glad to get back to fourth grade. Daddy remembers on another occasion Mr. Petterfield came down to quiz the students in our class. Two questions stand out in his mind. One was to spell the word "answer." Daddy somehow knew it was not just "a-n-s-e-r," but he could not remember how to spell it. So, for the first and only time, to the best of his recollection, he cheated. He looked over to the girl sitting next to him and copied her correct spelling. That was a very sad experience.

The other question the teacher asked was, "Which is heavier, a pound of gold or a pound of feathers?" Of course many students put a pound of gold. Other students put that they were the same weight. That was the answer which Daddy gave. I do not remember any of the students getting the correct answer. You see, the pound of feathers is heavier than the pound of gold because feathers are weighed upon the scale of sixteen ounces to the pound but all precious metals are weighed on the troy scale of twelve ounces to the pound. Thus no matter how light feathers are, a pound of feathers still would be four ounces heavier than the pound of gold.

At the end of 4A class both Uncle Russell and Daddy were promoted to 5A. However, we knew that we would not be at Cardiff Public School the next year because, after the death of Great-grandma Bailey in October, it was decided that our family would move back to the family home in Hamilton where we had lived for the first eighteen months of our lives. There we would care for Grandma's father, Great-grandpa John Oliver Bailey, who was then 77 years of age. In making this decision, Grandma was honoring the Lord's plan for children to care for their parents in their old age and infirmities and to be willing to fulfill their wishes as Joseph did for his father Jacob.

> And the time drew nigh that Israel must die: and he called his son Joseph, and said unto him, If now I have found grace in thy sight, put, I pray thee, thy hand under my thigh, and deal kindly and truly with me; bury me not, I pray thee, in Egypt: but I will lie with my fathers, and thou shalt carry me out of Egypt, and bury me in their buryingplace. And he said, I will do as thou hast said. And he said, Swear unto me. And he sware unto him. And Israel bowed himself upon the bed's head. Genesis 47:29–31

Chapter 16

The Second World War

When Uncle Russell and Daddy had not quite reached six years of age, the Second World War began. Germany, led by Adolph Hitler, had been conquering a number of nations, including Austria and Czechoslovakia. In 1938, Great Britain's Prime Minister, Neville Chamberlain, had met with Adolph Hitler and a number of other European leaders in Munich, Germany, hoping that they could stop Hitler's aggressive takeover of other nations. However, in September of 1939, Hitler moved his armed forces into Poland, and Britain was no longer willing to allow this aggression to continue. When the Prime Minister announced to the House of Commons in London that Hitler had aggressively sent his army and military equipment into Poland, they declared war against Germany.

It was only ten hours later in the House of Parliament in Canberra, Australia, that Robert Gordon Menzies, the Prime Minister of Australia declared, "Great Britain is at war; therefore Australia is at war." As in the Boer War and the First World War, the loyalty of Australia to the "mother country" (Great Britain) was such that this support was provided without the least hesitation. It seemed almost immediately that young men were conscripted into the army.

We, especially Grandma, were afraid that Grandpa, then 27 years of age, would be conscripted into the army. He was saved by two situations. When he was called up to register for the army, he was given a "B" health classification because they thought he had rheumatoid arthritis. He was also working as an employee of the New South Wales Government Railway. This was a very high priority job because of the necessity to keep the tracks in top condition for the movement of troops, war supplies, food, ammunition, transport vehicles, and other war equipment. It was essential to keep the railroad tracks in good repair. For these two reasons Grandpa was not conscripted into the army, and to this day we thank God for that.

However, these were very difficult and frightening times. At the time, Australia had a population of only 7,000,000. The Japanese, who entered the war in 1941, had built a very powerful military and had many more citizens in their nation. At that time, Australia fully believed that Japan had its focus on Australia, thinking it would be a wonderful place to which Japan could expand.

We watched and listened in amazement when we saw all the changes which were taking place. Many young men, and some not so young, were sent over to Europe to help Britain in Europe and North Africa, where some of the fiercest battles took place. However, when on December 7, 1941, the Japanese attacked Pearl Harbor, things changed dramatically for the worse. While our troops were fighting in Europe and North Africa, there was no thought that Australia might ever be attacked. But once the Japanese joined the Axis powers led by Germany, there was ever a possibility, indeed a probability, that their goal would include an attack upon Australia.

I remember the fear which Uncle Russell and Daddy felt as eight-year-olds. We saw a great change in what was taking place in our school. Trenches about three feet deep were very quickly dug around the perimeter of the playground of the Cardiff public school, and we practiced running to these trenches and either kneeling or crouching down should any attack come to our area. We were trained that whenever a plane flew over, we were not to question whether it was a friendly plane or a Japanese plane. We were to run into the trenches and there wait until the plane had passed by. If we were not where there were trenches—perhaps on the playing field during Wednesday afternoon's sports time—we were to lie flat on the ground with our head buried inside our folded arms.

Then there were the practicing times. Every parent received a note asking them to set their watches or clocks exactly to radio time, for as soon as school was dismissed for the day, the children were to run home as fast as they could and then the parent was to indicate through a note to the principal the exact time the children arrived home. Grandma told Uncle Russell and Daddy to run home as fast as they possibly could. However, we were some distance away from the school. We did run as fast as we could, and we were fast runners. Both of us had even been chosen to represent our school in running. But, because of the distance, we had taken longer than allowed by the school, and we were told that we had to stay at the school if there was any sound of an alarm. When we reported this to Grandma, she disagreed and said, "No matter what the teachers say, you are to run home because I want to know were you are." Providentially, we never did have to follow that instruction. Quickly, Grandpa dug an air raid shelter by hand where the family could hide if the Japanese were to bomb the region. When we think how fragile the roof of that air raid shelter was, it would have taken only a very tiny bomb to penetrate the air raid shelter.

It was about this time that Grandpa was made a warden in our area. The wardens were assigned to assist anyone injured by a Japanese attack. Uncle Russell and Daddy remember as little boys going to the fire station one night not far from where we lived. There the wardens demonstrated a tiny version of an incendiary bomb—a bomb designed to burn down buildings by exploding into flames on impact. While it was a rather small device, nevertheless, it looked as if it could be a very dangerous weapon. The wardens demonstrated how such a device could be put out, if action were taken immediately. Grandpa was issued with a gas mask, a piece of equipment important for all rescuers. It had to be located in a very accessible place in our house so that it could be used immediately if needed. By the grace of God it never was used. However, as boys Uncle Russell and Daddy would sometimes put the mask on, for it was intriguing to us.

During the war time, there were at least four fires which were started by an arsonist in the Cardiff area. All the fires were lit at nighttime and occurred in buildings which were unoccupied at the time of the fire. Two fires were in unoccupied houses; one was at what we called a picture theater (a movie house or cinema); and the fourth was in the

Roman Catholic school. As the Roman Catholic school was very close to where we lived, we all were called out of bed when we heard the fire sirens, and, quickly putting coats on, we went up to watch the terrible fire. In some ways, as boys, it seemed very exciting to see such a fire. While we were watching, one of the Catholic ladies fainted, apparently so overcome with grief that the school was being burned to the ground. To the best of our recollection that was the first time I had ever seen somebody faint.

Some months later, a young man was taken into the police station and charged with the arson of the buildings. Wherever happened to him we did not learn.

War is a dreadful thing, for many innocent people lose their lives, and many have no more opportunity to turn to the Lord for His salvation. War had its origins in heaven, and Satan still delights in war.

> And the great dragon was cast out, that old serpent, called the Devil, and Satan, which deceiveth the whole world: he was cast out into the earth, and his angels were cast out with him. Revelation 12:9

Chapter 17

Attending Boolaroo Church From Our Home in Cardiff

After our move from Boolaroo to live in Cardiff in 1939, it was no longer a short walk to the Boolaroo church, which was still the closest church to where we lived. There was a good bus service between Newcastle and Boolaroo which passed right by our front gate. However, we were not unmindful of the cost. Being still confined to the small salary Grandpa earned, every effort was made to save literally every penny. The cost of the fare from Cardiff to Boolaroo was three pence (two and one-half cents) for adults and a penny for children. With return fares that would amount to one shilling four pence (thirteen cents), for Grandpa, Grandma, Uncle Russell, and Daddy.

Our parents did everything they could to be frugal. Just prior to our move, after much careful saving, Grandpa had been able to purchase a brand new bicycle. It was green in color and had been made in Boolaroo by a man named Mr. Warwick and so the name of the bike was Warwick. Grandma and Grandpa devised a plan whereby that one shilling and four pence would be reduced to eight pence (a little less than seven cents). The plan was simple. Grandpa would ride his bike to Boolaroo church, and he would double either Uncle Russell or Daddy on the bike. This was by no means an easy task, for just after we crossed the bridge over the railway tracks there was a steep hill descending to the center of the town of Cardiff. It was too steep to risk pedaling down, especially with one of Grandpa's boys sitting sidewise on the bicycle bar. Even the rest of the journey was not always easy for Grandpa because there were some smaller inclines and declines. However, when we came to the street to turn up to the church, again we had to dismount from the bike because it was too steep for Grandpa to pedal up the hill. That street was covered with gravel, and it ended just beside the church.

After the afternoon youth service (Missionary Volunteer meeting), Grandpa would then double the other one of us home. He would ride down the street from the church until he came to the main road. Well Daddy remembers, on one occasion when he was the one to ride home while Uncle Russell went home on the double-decker bus with Grandma. As we were coming slowly down the hill with Grandpa applying the brakes, somehow Daddy carelessly allowed the heel of his shoe to hit the spokes of the front wheel of the bike, and we both toppled over. Both of us bled a little from superficial wounds, and Grandpa was not happy with Daddy. He warned me to never again allow my feet to move backwards. Daddy heeded that warning, and never again did it happen. Of course, Uncle Russell also had a similar warning, and he was able to avoid the same fate.

In those days almost all the people, young and old, stayed at the church between the church service and the start of the Missionary Volunteer Meeting. Even though these meetings were directed to young people, most of the older people were also interested in listening to the meetings. Of course, at the Boolaroo church there were hardly any young people, and Uncle Russell and Daddy were small children; therefore, we were not counted as even junior missionary volunteers. However, we learned much from these meetings.

Because most people stayed after the church service, every family would bring a sandwich lunch and maybe some fruit. There was always time after we had eaten lunch, and, as active boys, Uncle Russell and Daddy wanted to do different things. Especially in the warmer weather we would leave the grounds of the church, usually accompanied by an older child or an adult, and we would go farther up the grassy hill and sometimes look over the town of Boolaroo below. It was more interesting in the springtime when quite a few different wild flowers were in bloom. We would see how many different flowers we could find, and, as I remember, most of the flowers were white, yellow, pink, or purple.

One of the most difficult times for Uncle Russell and Daddy at Boolaroo church was during communion service. Being active boys, we knew the service would be much longer than usual, and that was a test. However, there was compensation. When the adults went either downstairs or into the little foyer of the church for the foot-washing part of the service, someone would stay back to tell the children a story. We certainly looked forward to this. The real test came later when the emblems of the communion service were served. We would look with longing eye upon the communion bread and wine, only wishing that we could participate, too. In that time, the Seventh-day Adventist Church practiced "closed communion"—that is, it was only for baptized Seventh-day Adventist members who participated in the service. If there were visitors who were not Seventh-day Adventists, they were always welcomed, of course. They were invited to observe the foot-washing ceremony, but they did not participate in it; neither did they receive of the unleavened bread—the symbol of the broken body of Jesus—nor of the unfermented wine—the symbol of His spilled blood.

Of course, because children were not baptized they did not participate, and that was appropriate, for they had not yet made their commitment to Christ. It pains Uncle Russell and Daddy today to see little children being served the communion emblems when they have little understanding of its significance. It is a very solemn service in which to participate, and there are very great admonitions in 1 Corinthians chapter 11 to those who participate in the communion service unworthily. The communion is a time for special prayer, special searching of heart, and special putting away of sin as we confess and repent of any sins which we have in our lives and making reconciliation with anyone with whom we have had misunderstandings. Daddy wants his children to remember how important it is to prepare their hearts for the communion service.

> For he that eateth and drinketh unworthily, eateth and drinketh damnation to himself, not discerning the Lord's body. 1 Corinthians 11:29

Chapter 18

A Miracle That Saved Uncle Russell's Life

It was early October of 1942, just before we had turned nine and only a few days before Grandma Bailey died. Outside of traveling to South Australia to visit Grandpa's relatives, the only vacation which we took was a one-week vacation to the beautiful, rugged Blue Mountains, about 60 miles west of Sydney. It was meant to be a very special treat and so in many ways it was.

We were fascinated to meet a man who was an Austrian. Austria was united with Germany at that time in fighting against the Allies, which included Australia during the Second World War. This man, therefore, was a citizen of an enemy nation. Somehow he had been allowed to remain without being put in a concentration camp with other people in Australia who were considered a threat to Australia's security. However, he told us that he had to report to the police every day. He fascinated us with his stories of being a prisoner of the Russians during the First World War. In spite of his past experience in a Russian prisoner-of-war camp, he told us that the most beautiful language he had ever heard was the Russian language. We were also intrigued that whenever we saw him, he had an unlit cigarette in his mouth. Grandma eventually asked him why he was doing this, and he explained that he was trying to give up smoking, and somehow it was easier if he had an unlit cigarette in his mouth. I certainly hope that he succeeded to break this very unhealthful habit.

One morning, as a special treat, Grandpa and Grandma decided to take us to the scenic railway. It was quite a long walk, maybe two miles from the little room in which we were staying. However, when we arrived, we were shocked at its appearance. It did not have regular carriages; in fact, it had open carriages which had only two-foot-high sides, the carriage seats were at an angle slanting backwards, and there was no engine. We did see a huge steel cable attached to the back of this train of three or four carriages. We got into the train, and they strapped us tightly into our seats. The train slowly began to move, and then suddenly it began to race down the mountain side, probably traveling 2,000 or 3,000 feet to the valley at the bottom of the mountain. Uncle Russell and Daddy were scared out of their wits, and we were so thankful when we could get out of the carriage.

Then we were to walk perhaps another five miles along the valley until we came to what was called the Giant Staircase. It was more than 2,000 steps up to the top of the mountain. Uncle Russell and Daddy have never seen a staircase like that any other time in our lives.

We had walked perhaps three miles or so when we came to a very high, narrow waterfall which came from the top of the mountain down into the valley. A little wooden bridge had been constructed in front of the waterfalls so that hikers could all pass over safely to the other side. We were all tired, and we decided to rest a little while to be refreshed by the spray from the waterfall.

Daddy sat on the bridge close to the pathway, and Uncle Russell tried to walk around me. Somehow, suddenly he slipped, perhaps because of the wet spray, and down he went. If he had fallen to the bottom, no doubt he would have been killed because it was about 90 feet to the rocks below. To this day we believe it was the angels who miraculously got his little hands around the diagonal wooden support which connected the bottom of the bridge to the solid ground. He grasped this support with both hands, holding on tightly and dangling 90 feet above the rocks.

Immediately Grandma cried out, "Hang on, Russy! Hang on!" Grandpa immediately got down on his abdomen and was stretching down to get hold of Uncle Russell's wrists while Grandma and Daddy held on to Grandpa's legs to try to make sure that he did not fall over. Eventually he reached Uncle Russell's wrists, and, after getting a strong grip, he lifted him up to the bridge.

You can imagine the very earnest prayer that Grandpa prayed as we all knelt in the dust of the path to thank God for His protection. How wonderful God was to Uncle Russell, for He was protecting him and saving him for the ministry to which God had called him and that he has fulfilled to this day! How happy Daddy is that nothing happened to Uncle Russell that day!

Yes, we walked to the top of the Giant Staircase. It was hard, and it took us a long time, and we were very tired when we got home, but still we were so happy that nothing happened to destroy the life of Uncle Russell. This was the first of a number of times we were aware that God intervened to save either Uncle Russell's or Daddy's life. We must every day place our lives in the hands of Jesus. I always remember the words of Pastor Eric B. Hare when he told us what his American mother said, just before he and his young bride were leaving Melbourne for seven years of mission service in Burma: "Eric, remember, you are immortal until your work is done."

Always remember that God protects His faithful young people—even little children and youth.

> They shall bear thee up in their hands, lest thou dash thy foot against a stone. Psalm 91:12

> The angel of the Lord encampeth round about them that fear him, and delivereth them. Psalm 34:7

CHAPTER 19

The Death of Great-grandma Bailey

Probably no single event in our childhood impacted more upon Uncle Russell and Daddy than the death of Great-grandma Alice Bailey. Great-grandma Bailey had been born in Newcastle, England and was brought to Australia in 1880 by her parents when she was nine years old, where they settled in the city of Newcastle, Australia.

No doubt because both cities were industrial cities, your Great-great-grandfather Craig was able to find work similar to that which he had been doing in England. Clearly Great-grandma Bailey had come from a very deeply religious home. She herself became a Primitive Methodist. This was a form of the Methodist Church which sought to keep the reforms which John Wesley had instituted in the eighteenth century. They believed the Methodist Church had lost its foundation and was drifting into worldliness. They had seen the gradual compromise of novel reading, card playing, and the introduction of dancing into the church halls. These amusements were denounced by the Primitive Methodists.

Great-grandma Bailey was a deeply converted woman with a very simple faith and trust in God. She contrasted with Great-grandpa Bailey, a man who was hardly ever found in a church except maybe for an occasional wedding or funeral. Remember Great-grandma Bailey who had first heard and accepted the Seventh-day Adventist message in our family. How Uncle Russell and Daddy thank the Lord for the wonderful courage which Jesus gave her! That provided a Christian environment for Grandma when she was born into the family twelve years later. Of course, Grandma was fervent in teaching Uncle Russell and Daddy the wonderful, blessed message which we know today.

Being the youngest child, Grandma had to help Great-grandma a lot. Great-grandma was more than 40 years old when Grandma was born. When Grandma was in the eighth grade and fourteen years of age, she received permission to leave school to help care for her ailing mother. When we were born, Great-grandma Bailey was already in her 60s. We knew her only as an older woman, but we soon learned to love her; she was kind, and she seemed to love us both very dearly. We loved it when she came to visit and also when we would go to visit her.

Even though she was only nine when she came to Australia, she still retained some of that English accent. On one occasion, being far more adventuresome than Great-grandpa Bailey, she decided to travel with us to South Australia to meet Grandpa's relatives, and she had a wonderful time there. That was the only time our two Great-grandmothers met.

However, when we were eight years of age, we learned that Great-grandma Bailey was very ill and that she had a serious problem with what they then called "dropsy." (Today her condition is called congestive heart failure.) We did not understand it very well, but we knew from what Grandma told us that Great-grandma's legs were filling up with "water" and making them swell very badly. We knew Grandma was very concerned about Great-grandma, and there seemed to be very little that the doctors of those days could do to help her. Every now and again we would hear that they "tapped" Great-grandma's legs. This was a procedure to allow the "water" to be taken out of her leg to give her some relief. That proved only to be a temporary relief. Grandma received word that Great-grandma was quickly deteriorating. So on a Friday afternoon, she traveled by bus to see Great-grandma, which was to be the last time she would see her alive.

By this time, Great-grandma was in a delirium, and she was calling out for Fred, her youngest son who had disappeared in 1922 when he was fifteen and was never heard from again. She was also directing her oldest son Great-uncle John Oliver (Great-uncle "Ol") to care for the baby. She was recalling some of the events in her past life. Grandma came home very concerned about the health of Great-grandma.

The next morning we were getting ready to go to Boolaroo church when Great-uncle Ol came to our house on his bicycle. It was a long and strenuous bike ride to come from Hamilton to Cardiff and Great-uncle Ol had never done that before. Before he could say anything, Grandma knew that Great-grandma had died. Great-grandma Bailey, at 71 years of age, was the first of any of our relatives that we knew who had died. It was an experience we found hard to understand. We attended her funeral held at the Moore's Funeral Home, where they sang Great-grandpa's favorite hymn, "Face to Face with Christ My Savior." After the service, we boarded the bus which was hired to take the mourners to the Sandgate Cemetery, the main cemetery for the city of Newcastle, and there she was laid to rest to await the call of the Lifegiver.

The death of Great-grandma Bailey was to change the circumstances of our family dramatically. It was soon decided that the only one who was in a position to take care for Great-grandpa Bailey was Grandma. This she agreed to do. This meant moving from Cardiff to Hamilton. There were some positive aspects to this. The Bailey home, at 78 Dumaresq Street, was only a short distance from the Newcastle Seventh-day Adventist School which was then located on Kent Street, Hamilton, behind a small alcove of palm trees. There we were educated from the fifth grade to the eleventh grade, which was the end of high school in those days. After school finished in December 1942, we said "goodbye" to our friends at Cardiff School, and the family moved in with Great-grandpa Bailey.

Uncle Russell and Daddy did not look forward to this move because we were so afraid of Great-grandpa Bailey. We knew that he had no toleration for active, noisy little boys. He had made that very plain on the visits we had made to our Great-grandparents' home. We had reason to be afraid, for living with Great-grandpa all the time meant frequent outbursts about our noisiness, about our carelessly allowing the doors to slam, and all sorts of other minor and more major situations which angered Great-grandfather greatly.

We were now in our new school and we had much adjustment to make. We had gone from a sizeable public school with only one grade in each classroom, to a situation where all six primary grades were in the same classroom, taught by a young teacher, Judy Lane. She was a reasonably nice teacher, but we succeeded in getting into various little issues which led us to be disciplined. That carried on for a number of years. One form of punishment in those days was the use of a cane. The erring student was required to hold out his hand and the teacher would hit one hand with the cane, then the other. The number of strokes (or "cuts") of the cane one would receive depended upon the severity of the offense. For the very worst offenses, the maximum penalty was six "cuts" of the cane.

For our first three weeks at the school, Mr. Ivy was the principal. We soon learned that he had a reputation for punishing harshly. Something had already happened with Daddy that led Miss Lane to tell him that he had to go to Mr. Ivy's office. Daddy was terrified because of what he had heard about Mr. Ivy, and he pled with her to give him another chance. This she did. After three weeks, Mr. Ivy was sent to another school, and 24-year-old Robert Henry Parr became the new principal. While we learned to like him very much, nevertheless, he seemed no less reluctant to use the cane on disobedient boys than had Mr. Ivy, and both Uncle Russell and Daddy received quite a few strokes of the cane. However, we never did receive more than four "cuts" of the cane, indicating we were not thought to be guilty of the most severe form of misbehavior. It took us quite a while to get used to the multi-grade classes. We would be distracted by what was taking place in the other classes; however, we eventually got used to it, and it was no longer a problem for us.

We now attended the much larger Hamilton church, the biggest Seventh-day Adventist church in the Newcastle area. The church was located six blocks from where we lived. We were also within a relatively lengthy walk to the bottom of the shopping center of Newcastle—very helpful to Grandma when she went shopping. There was also a reasonably good shopping center in Hamilton itself, where all the fruits and vegetables were supplied. This was different from Cardiff, where Grandma had bought fruit and vegetables from "the green grocer," a man who sold fruit and vegetables from home to home with a horse and cart. However, horses and carts were still commonly used in Newcastle. Eventually, we purchased a little ice chest to keep a few things cool. The ice man would come regularly with the blocks of ice in a covered cart drawn by a horse. The baker from Cann's Bakery also went door to door selling bread from a covered horse-drawn cart.

The same thing happened early in the morning where we put out our "Billy can" (a metal tin can with a lid) and money every night, and the milkman would provide us with milk early in the morning. I do not remember that money being stolen even once, though on rare occasions we did hear that someone's milk money had been stolen.

Of course, there were also some automobiles, but very few people owned cars, as these were the war years, and petrol (gasoline) was very much in short supply. Those who had cars received special tickets which would be used every month to allow them to buy a little gasoline. There were some who put large gas producers on the top of their cars, but that was a very poor form of fuel for the vehicles, and the cars often did not work well.

Other coupons were given to all the citizens of Australia, limiting what could be purchased. We had coupons for clothing, with each garment designated to account for a certain number of coupons. Obviously, small items required less coupons than, say, a suit. We also received coupons for meat, but we did not use them. We did not use the tea coupons either, but there were always people wanting to receive our tea coupons. Probably there were wealthy people who were able to get around these great restrictions, but it certainly was a way to keep people from overspending.

There were no such things as credit cards in Australia in those days. Neither did most people have checkbooks. It was cash all the way. Though Grandpa had a small salary, it was very adequate, as rationing limited what we could buy. There was also a ration on butter. Well I remember how Grandma would divide the butter into four equal parts, and each of us would have our own little ration. Each of us was allowed six ounces of butter a week. No doubt Grandma realized that her boys would take more than their fair share if it was not equally divided out.

There was no good margarine at that time. Many people used drippings (animal fat) on their bread, but, of course, we did not do that. There was a product called "copha," a white spread made from coconut oil. It was very dry and flakey and did not spread well. Eventually, Meadow-Lea was manufactured. Colored like butter, it was probably also made primarily from coconut oil with some other different ingredients. It was also very flakey and hard, if not impossible, to spread; however, we began to use some of these alternate products.

This was a world far removed from today's world, but in many ways the simpler life was also much less stressful. It was a wonderful time to practice the Scripture's counsel to be content with your lot.

> . . . I have learned, in whatsoever state I am, therewith to be content. Philippians 4:11

Chapter 20

School Life at the Seventh-day Adventist School

The first Seventh-day Adventist school we attended was an intermediate school—that is, it had six grades of primary education and three grades of high school education. This would take students to the ninth grade, after which, if they desired to continue school, they would transfer to a public school in Newcastle. This worried your Grandparents, especially Grandma, who did not want Uncle Russell and Daddy to go to public schools. She realized they were not the place for her boys to receive a Christian education. Later, the school added the final two years of high school, making it the Newcastle Seventh-day Adventist High School. Yet in all the seven years we studied in that school, it never did reach 50 students in all eleven grades.

In the early days of attending this school, it was very difficult for Uncle Russell and Daddy. The playground was ruled by a strong, very active, fifteen-year-old boy we knew only as "Bunny" Lane. Bunny was the younger brother of Judy Lane, our first teacher when we were in fifth grade. Because we were only nine and there were other small children like us, Bunny Lane took charge and controlled whatever we did.

For example, there was an air-raid shelter which had been built in the school. For some reason, Bunny wanted more of the sandy soil dug out, and he would send the little boys into the shelter to get buckets of sand and pass them out, and then he would scatter the sand elsewhere. It was very dangerous indeed because at any time there could have been such a fall of sand that it would have buried a child. Providentially, that did not happen. None of us dared disregard Bunny's demands. He was our first recollection of a real bully.

Bunny had an assistant in his work—fourteen-year-old Gordon Craig who, we were to discover many years later, was Mother's second cousin. He was not a bully like Bunny; however, he was often given the orders from Bunny to bring the children Bunny wanted to work for him. One time Bunny decided that he was going to grow a garden in the school yard. Of course, this was not a bad thing in itself, but Bunny ruled the playground by fear, and he became the taskmaster while the rest of us did whatever he asked us to do. For some reason, no action was taken by the school.

Robert Craig, a younger brother of Gordon, was a little older than us, and he was a student in our same class. On one occasion, Robert apparently had not done what Bunny had told him to do, and Bunny hit him across the ear. This was reported to the principal, Mr. Parr. As we were lined up for assembly which we did every day outside the school building (unless it was raining), Mr. Parr addressed the issue and asked, "Bunny, did you hit 'Mus' Craig?" ("Mus" was his nickname given by Mr. Parr because Bob was not a very strong youngster. It seemed that it was a slight to his physical weakness.) "Did you hit 'Mus' Craig on the ear?" We were all shocked when Bunny responded, "Yes, and I would do it again."

We looked to Mr. Parr to see what action he would take. But to the best of our knowledge, no action was taken. That made us even more afraid of Bunny because we felt we had no protection from our young principal. Of course, Bunny was the younger brother of our first teacher. Whether that played into the situation we do not know. Thankfully, he left at the end of the year. At the same time, his sister was transferred to another appointment, and she was replaced by another young lady teacher, Lila Robb. Miss Robb was not as dignified a young woman as was Judy Lane, who was a petite and very gracious young lady. Judy Lane was an adopted daughter, and the father of the Lanes was a Seventh-day Adventist minister who was a chaplain in the Australian Army. Like Bunny, he was of a very strong physical build.

On another occasion the situation deteriorated so badly that quite a number of students, including Uncle Russell and Daddy, fled from the school grounds and hid in the streets a long distance from the school as Bunny tried to find us. We waited a long time until we knew the classes would be in session again. Then we timidly returned to the school grounds and to the class. Mr. Parr demanded to know why we were so late for classes. We forget now whether we actually told him the real reason we were always so much afraid of Bunny.

Uncle Russell and Daddy have not forgotten some of the dismal results we received in our primary final at the end of sixth grade, which determined whether we would be promoted into the seventh grade (the first of the high school grades). Both of us received zero out of twenty for spelling; both received two and one-half out of twenty for art. Providentially, we had done well in all the other subjects, however, so this did not prevent us from being promoted to the high school. We felt very proud now to be high school students. We were especially pleased that we no longer studied art or spelling for examinations. We were also happy that the teachers were all men. Somehow we preferred men teachers to women teachers.

At the time there were two male teachers in the high school—Mr. Robert Parr and Mr. Walter Hill. Mr. Hill was a quite different man from Mr. Parr—somewhat older, of small build and of sensitive disposition, but generally speaking, a kindly man. On the other hand, Mr. Parr was ever the strong, but pleasant leadership type. We greatly admired him. He seemed to be at his best in handling boys (Bunny excepted). He was considerably more outgoing than Mr. Hill, who we respected, however.

Later, Winston Dunlop joined the staff. He had finished the Newcastle Adventist School at the end of ninth grade when there was no tenth or eleventh grade and he had to complete his studies at Newcastle Boy's High School. He had graduated two years before us and had been brought back to be a junior teacher. It was hard for us to get used to calling him Mr. Dunlop rather than Winston or "Win" as we normally called him. He was a talented young man but he taught Uncle Russell and Daddy no classes because economics was the only class he taught in the advanced high school area, and we did not study economics.

While the Newcastle Seventh-day Adventist school was far from perfect, nevertheless, it was far better than the public school. However, Uncle Russell and Daddy now wish it would have followed all the true principles of Christian education. All children and youth need all the help which true Christian education provides. This education is invaluable to children and youth who are taught by men and women who themselves are taught by the Holy Spirit.

> But the Comforter, which is the Holy Ghost, whom the Father will send in my name, he shall teach you all things, and bring all things to your remembrance, whatsoever I have said unto you. John 14:26

Chapter 21

Trigger

When Uncle Russell and Daddy were boys, we longed to have a dog. Because we lived in a suburban area of the city of Newcastle, Grandma and Grandpa were reluctant for us to have a dog. Eventually, Grandma could see how much we would love to have such a pet, so she told us to go to the animal shelter of the RSPCA (Royal Society for the Prevention of Cruelty to Animals). We did not take a second telling, and we rode our bikes the couple of miles to the nearest RSPCA animal shelter. There were quite a few dogs there; however, one black dog really took our fancy. When we approached his cage, he came running toward us and seemed such a friendly dog. He appeared to be young but probably fully grown.

We found out that the RSPCA would sell him to us for 5 shillings (50 cents). That was not a small amount when we were boys, but in spite of that we rushed back to Grandma and said, "He only costs five shillings." However, mother asked another question, "How big is he? I don't want a big dog." We said, "He is a little bigger than a Fox Terrier." In fact, he was considerably bigger than a Fox Terrier. He was a black Kelpie. Now the Kelpie dog was bred in Australia to be a sheep dog, and they come in two colors, black and ginger. We have heard that in their breeding there is some Dingo, the wild dog of Australia. Indeed they make excellent sheep dogs. In the end, mother gave us the five shillings to buy him and lead him back home on a leash.

Mother was very surprised to see how big the dog was. She thought about how much it would cost to feed this dog, but nevertheless she permitted us to keep the dog. Grandpa seemed to be neutral about our having the dog. One thing that very quickly displeased Grandpa and Grandma was the fact that he barked often, and they were afraid that the neighbors would be disturbed or upset. However, I do not remember any of our neighbors complaining.

Uncle Russell and Daddy were so happy to have their first dog. When we were younger we had a cat, but we thought dogs were much better pets than cats. We called our dog Trigger. Many people told us that Trigger was a horse's name, not a dog's name, but still we liked the name Trigger and he soon learned his name. He was such a good dog. When we arrived home from school he would be waiting at the gate for us, wagging his tail very vigorously when he saw us or heard our voices. He certainly became "our" dog, even though he responded to others.

To feed the dog we had to buy dog's meat from the butcher shop. The butcher shop was several blocks away from where we lived, but we would buy scraps of meat and bones for Trigger. We were still in the war years, for we were 10 or 11 years old at this time. After several purchases at the butcher's shop, the butcher expressed his displeasure that we were buying dog meat but not buying meat from him for the family. It was at the time when many things were rationed by the government, including meat, so that each family could only buy a limited amount of meat. Of course we did not use the meat tickets. We told the butcher that we did not eat meat. He seemed to be skeptical, but we assured him that we were vegetarians and did not eat meat. Then he asked, "What do you do with your tickets?" We answered, "Nothing." So he asked us if we would bring our tickets to him, which we did. That made him very happy. We do not know what he did with those tickets, but perhaps he used them for his family, or maybe he gave them to friends, relatives, or good customers.

Trigger soon developed a bad habit. Our street did not have many cars passing by because there were few cars in Australia in the first half of the 1940s. However when one came, and if he could get over the fence, he would chase the car, barking vigorously at it in a very dangerous way so that we were always afraid that he might be killed. Indeed one day he was very close to being killed. Somehow he got in front of the car and the car went right over him, however he was between the four wheels of the car. He got hurt somewhat because, being the sized dog he was, he was hit by some of the metal under the car. Nevertheless, he had no permanent injuries or broken bones.

We always had laying hens in a pen. Mother would have us sell their eggs for her Sabbath school investment program. From time to time father would buy day-old chicks from the pet store in Newcastle. He had built a little pen for these chickens. One Sabbath, somehow, either Uncle Russell or Daddy, when feeding the chickens, had left the little gate open and this allowed the chickens to leave the pen when they were still very small. We knew nothing about this mistake until we returned home from church at lunch time. There was Trigger trying to round the chickens up into the pen. He still had the instincts of a dog trying to round up sheep, but obviously trying to round up chickens was an entirely different task. He was running after them and trying his best to round them back towards the pen, but somehow they were not easy to control, and one would run in one direction and one in another. He did not hurt any of them; he was just doing what his breed of dog was bred to do. We were quite impressed with his efforts, unsuccessful though they were. However he did keep the chickens from wandering far away.

Yet, his behavior became less acceptable. Sometimes, when he would be with us, no doubt in great efforts to protect us, he would bark rather menacingly at other people. Never did he bite or seriously attack someone, but some people became afraid of him because of the loudness of his bark. This was certainly true of a tiny old man, Jimmy Pike. Jimmy Pike had been a famous man in his day. He was a race horse jockey, and twice he had ridden the Melbourne Cup winner in his younger days.

Now, only Australians and New Zealanders would know what the Melbourne Cup race is. The Melbourne Cup is the most famous horse race in Australia, and it is run every year on the first Tuesday of November—the same day Americans have their main election day. The winning horse, its owners, and its jocky become instantaneous celebrities in Australia each year. The Melbourne Cup is a far more famous race in Australia than, for example, the Kentucky Derby is in the United States.

In the state of Victoria, they actually have a public holiday in honor of the Melbourne Cup day. The vast majority of the Australians stop work to watch or to listen on radio to the running of the Melbourne Cup. People who would not place bets on horses any other time of the year will take part in a race pool, where people will pick out of a hat the name of a horse, and of course the one who holds the name of the winning horse receives the money which has been contributed. Having won the race twice, Jimmy Pike was a well-known identity, not only in his home city of Newcastle but all over Australia and New Zealand.

When Mr. Pike would go for his daily stroll, Trigger would see him and would bark furiously at him, and Mr. Pike being very small and now very old became very afraid. Using very bad language, Mr. Pike said to us, "If he ever touches me, I will sue you and your parents." That was more than Grandpa could accept. Whether it would have happened we do no know, but at that moment Grandpa decided that he would take Trigger back to the pound at RSPCA where we had bought him. We had not had him for a full year then, but we were greatly distressed. We pleaded with Grandpa, but to no avail. He got on his bicycle, called to Trigger and Trigger followed him dutifully all the way to the pound.

We often wondered what happened to Trigger. Did some other kindly person or family buy him from the pound or would he, like so many stray animals, have been put to death? I know that for many days Uncle Russell and Daddy grieved over the loss of Trigger. We understood Grandpa's concern, but we really did not want to lose a dog which had become such a friend to us. It is always sad to lose a pet, and usually they are lost through death.

If you decide to have pets, you should treat them kindly and well, while training them to learn to obey so that they will not do things which are destructive or hurtful to other creatures, including humans. Remember, pets do not have the opportunity of eternal life as you do, but kindness to pets is a characteristic of true Christians who one day will live with Jesus in Heaven.

Chapter 22

Dishonesty

Sadly, when Uncle Russell and Daddy were little boys about 7 years old, we began to practice dishonesty. It happened a few times in Cardiff. To make a little money, Grandma would clean the baby health center in Cardiff. It was very close to where we lived. One day as Grandma was cleaning the clinic, Uncle Russell and Daddy went down to the clinic, and there we saw a little jar with money in it. We quickly took the jar, and when we counted the money we were amazed, for there was more than five shillings (more than 50 cents) in small coins in the jar.

At the time, the big craze at the Cardiff school was playing marbles. So we decided we would spend all the money on buying marbles. When we had the opportunity, unbeknown to Grandma, we went down to the shopping center at the bottom of the hill, and there we put all the money down to buy marbles. I believe that bought more than 200 marbles. We had never seen so many marbles in all our lives. Now we knew we were going to have a lot of fun. Of course, we hid the marbles so mother would not see them, and we took some to school.

When other students saw these brand-new marbles, everyone wanted to play us to win those marbles from us. At the time, we were only in third grade. Some of the older children in fifth and sixth grades did everything to cheat them from us. For example, one of the favorite games was called "pot the hole." A small shallow hole was dug with our hands. The two players would each put in the same number of marbles into the hand of one of the players. The one would try to throw them into the hole from a little distance away. Of course, our marbles were much newer than the other marbles, some of which would be chipped. When the marbles were thrown, if the number which went into the hole was an even number, then the thrower got all the marbles. If it was an odd number, the other player would get all the marbles. Quickly, after our throw, the other boy who was right at the hole would count, and if it was an even number he would flick another marble into the hole and say they were all his because there was an odd number in the hole. Because these were bigger boys, there was nothing we could do about it, and the pressure was on us to keep playing. Of course, we knew we were being cheated, but somehow we did not know how to avoid playing, and soon we were losing many of these marbles.

It did not take but a few days before all those marbles had been lost to other children. No doubt that was merited punishment for our terrible dishonesty. However, somehow, as mothers do, Grandma had found some of the marbles before we lost them all, and she demanded to know where we had gotten the marbles from, knowing that we had no money of our own. As is so often the case, when you commit one sin, you follow it up with another sin of lying, and, sadly, that is what Uncle Russell and Daddy did. We told Grandma that the woman down at the store had given us some marbles. Grandma was not convinced, so she decided to take us down to the store and ask the woman if it was true that she had given us these marbles. We were terrified, of course, knowing what the consequences would be if Grandma found out the real truth. We hurried on ahead of Grandma and then came back to tell her that the woman who had given us the marbles was not in the store. Grandma accepted that, and, with great relief, we were thankful that we had avoided the sure consequences of the punishment we would have received had Grandma learned the truth. However, Grandma assured us that we would go down again when the woman was there to find out whether those marbles had been given to us.

Grandma mentioned the situation to another lady, and this lady said to her, "Oh, they are very generous there. They gave a treat to my child once." Grandma accepted that as evidence that we were telling the truth, and we never did go down to face the consequences which we should have justly received from the sins which we had committed. However, many other wrongs that we did were more than adequately punished.

On another occasion, we found a bank book of some little boy. This would have been a bank account with the school bank. We thought this was wonderful, for we now had a bank account which showed there was money in the account, so, at an appropriate opportunity, we went to the bank to ask for the money to be taken out of the account. However, we were told that only Grandma could authorize money to be taken out of that account. Of course, the man at the bank believed that it was our personal account. That was a great disappointment to us. For some time, we hid the bank book in a crevice in the big Masonic Temple which was not too far from our home. After a while, we took the bank book back to near where we had found it, and we left it there when no one was observing. Whatever ultimately happened, Uncle Russell and Daddy do not know, but we certainly hope the little boy got his bank book back. Maybe it was replaced by the bank.

While Uncle Russell and Daddy did not steal very many times, it was not because of a lack of desire; rather, there were few opportunities to steal. One of our worst stealing efforts involved the thirteenth Sabbath mission offering jar. As you know, our family was very poor. Yet Grandma was always determined to have a special offering for the project every thirteenth Sabbath. Thus, every halfpenny Grandma received in change was put into this mission tin. The price of many items for sale in those days ended in a halfpenny. Therefore, over the period of thirteen weeks, there were many halfpennies which went into the mission tin. When thirteenth Sabbath came, Grandma always had several shillings to put into the thirteenth Sabbath mission offering, which was so much more than the regular sixpence (five cents) which Grandma and Grandpa would put in the regular Sabbath offering plate and the penny each which Uncle Russell and Daddy would put into the Sabbath school offering.

Somehow we found where the tin was hidden, and we started taking halfpennies out to buy sweets. One day Grandma realized that the number of halfpennies in the tin was much less than she had put in it. She immediately questioned Uncle Russell and Daddy, who once again did what so often happens when a sin is committed—we lied that we had not taken any such money. Apparently we were convincing enough for Grandma to believe us and to wonder if that money had been taken by the boy next door. Of course, that was never proven; however, Grandpa made sure that the tin was taken to a very secret place where no one would find it, and we never did find it.

Uncle Russell and Daddy occasionally stole things when we had opportunity until we were about twelve years of age. Somehow, we felt that we were not responsible for our actions. We had heard the importance of Jesus going to the temple when He was twelve years of age, and whatever we were taught we cannot fully remember, but it was in our minds that the parents stood for the salvation of their children before they were twelve. However, we believed that when we reached twelve years of age, we were then responsible before God for our salvation, and that brought a special desire in our hearts to stop stealing and doing other wrong things. We never stole again.

There were three other incidents of stealing which we remember. This was well after we had gone to live in Hamilton at age 9. One was taking off the teacher's table a small amount of money which belonged to a little girl in the class in Newcastle Seventh-day Adventist School. Also, by this time, we were absorbed in stamp collecting, and on a number of occasions when we were in Newcastle, we would go to the little kiosk in the arcade where a woman ran a small stamp-selling shop. Occasionally we bought some stamps if we were able to persuade Grandma to give us a penny or two. But we would ask to look through the stamp book, and if the woman's back was turned to us, we would quickly take a stamp or two out of the book and place it in our pockets. However, she caught us once and we never tried that again.

On another occasion, Grandma was given the responsibilities of arranging some floral decorations for the spring program at the Hamilton church. She wanted some gum tips—the very tender, amber-colored new leaves on gum trees early in the spring season—which made nice decorations. She gave Uncle Russell and Daddy two pence each so that we could catch the bus to travel beyond Cardiff to where there were many gum trees and pick the very nicest gum tips which we could find.

This we did, and we came back in the bus. We decided to leave the bus at Broadmeadow which was about one mile from where we lived. We went into a shop which sold comics. Of course, we had no money to buy comics, and indeed we had hardly ever read a comic book in our lives. Yet at that age we were tempted to see what was in these foolish comic books. We tried to steal one, but the lady saw us, and we ran as fast as we could, leaving the gum tips in the store. You can imagine Grandma's deep consternation when we returned without the gum tips. However, as usual, we tried to cover our tracks by lying, saying we had accidentally left the gum tips in the bus.

Uncle Russell and Daddy learned that when we did wrong we almost always tried to cover it up with another sin—the sin of lying. We believe that is why the Bible tells us that God's people who will be saved have no deceit, lies, or guile in their mouth.

> The remnant of Israel shall not do iniquity, nor speak lies; neither shall a deceitful tongue be found in their mouth: for they shall feed and lie down, and none shall make them afraid. Zephaniah 3:13

> And in their mouth was found no guile: for they are without fault before the throne of God. Revelation 14:5

Later in life, we asked for God's forgiveness through Jesus, and we paid into the Lord's work a much larger sum as restitution. We pray that all our readers will be strictly honest and truthful. If any have sinned in these ways, we entreat you not only to stop but to ask forgiveness and pay a larger amount in restitution to the person wronged where possible or to the Lord's work if it is not possible.

Chapter 23

JMVs and MVs

When we were young, we had JMV societies and MV societies. JMV stood for Junior Missionary Volunteer, and JMV meetings were held for children ages ten to fifteen. MV stood for Missionary Volunteer, and MV meetings were held for young people ages sixteen to thirty. These were meetings to train the children and youth for God's service. Daddy wishes that we had these today. It would be a great help to our children and young people growing up in church. Even when you were too young to join the Junior Missionary Society, you could be a Pal. When we first moved to Newcastle and became attendees at the Hamilton church, we were nine years old and we were Pals, for about one year.

The Junior Missionary Volunteer and the Missionary Volunteer societies permitted the young people to achieve advanced categories. There were four levels—Friends, Companions, Comrades (later Guides), and Master Comrades (Master Guides). However, to be a Master Comrade one had to be at least sixteen years of age. Uncle Russell and Daddy did not achieve that category because, very soon after we turned sixteen, we enrolled at Avondale College and did not complete all that was necessary to become a Master Comrade. We did complete the Friends, Companions and the Comrades requirements. These requirements were quite challenging and included Bible memory work, certain categories of service, reviewing parts of the Bible and the Spirit of Prophecy, participating in missionary work during the Sabbath hours, and fulfilling the requirements of various honors. These honors were in a number of categories, and one had to have completed a certain number of honors to progress from one stage to the next.

Meetings were held every Sabbath afternoon. The JMV meeting was held from 2:30 until 3:25 in the afternoon. They would be simple meetings, and some adults would also attend. The Juniors were able to participate actively in the running of the meetings. Each week we had a memory text to learn, and each one in the Junior Missionary Volunteer group was given the opportunity to recite the memory text for the week. An offering was taken and opportunity given where any mission service which had been undertaken during the week could be reported. We would report the number of person's helped, number of pieces of literature distributed, any clothes given to the needy, any money given to the needy and other such things. Uncle Russell and Daddy were always struggling to try to remember anything good they had done during the week so they would have something to report. The most common report was the number of people helped. Now this did not include doing the chores that children should be expected to do for their family. They had to be genuine acts which had been done to help others.

At 3:30 in the afternoon, the Missionary Volunteer meeting for the older young people commenced. However, we would all stay for it, and quite a few of the adult members of the church would be there, too, certainly including our parents. Many of the same activities followed—the taking up of missionary reports, collecting an offering, making helpful presentations about important things for young people, reciting the doctrinal text for that week and any similar activities. We loved those Sabbath afternoon activities, and Uncle Russell and Daddy are sorry that children today do not have these opportunities in most churches. It was a wonderful way to train children and youth to be workers for God and to serve Him with their hearts and minds. It was also a very profitable way to spend afternoon Sabbath hours. In winter time we would often close Sabbath before walking back from church to home.

We also had some very important lessons which we learned in our Vocational Honors. Uncle Russell and Daddy successfully completed a number of honors, but Daddy can remember only two of the honors which we received: one was in the study of animals, another in cycling.

In some ways Uncle Russell and Daddy really wondered whether we truly were worthy of the cycling honor. In that honor, young people had to be able to cycle 50 miles in a day under supervision, and they also had to learn how to do simple repairs such as mending a bike puncture and how to disassemble and to reassemble the parts of a bike. A young accountant at the North New South Wales Conference office, Milton Smith, agreed to be the one to take a group of about ten of us on the 50-mile ride for our cycling honor. We were up early on that Sunday morning. We rode to the flat-bottom barge which took cars across the Hunter River to the north side of the city of Newcastle. Then we rode our bikes on the road which led to Soldier's Point. Both Uncle Russell and Daddy had old, second-hand bikes which lacked all the help that modern bikes have today. We had no gears; therefore, it was very hard when we came to hills. We were about twelve years of age at the time; however, we did all we could, and we eventually covered the 25 miles in one direction. Then we turned back to complete the full 50 miles. That we did, but under very difficult circumstances. About nine miles before reaching back to the Hunter River again, Uncle Russell had a puncture in his back tire, and even though it might seem obvious that we should have taken a repair kit with us, no one had brought one.

Thus, Uncle Russell had to ride his bike with a flat back tire which certainly was not good for the tire or for the rim of the wheel. It was very hard, especially after such a long ride. When Uncle Russell felt he could not keep up, Daddy got on his bike and Uncle Russell got on Daddy's bike. It was very hard for Daddy also. Eventually, tired and very weary, we got back. We also completed the rest of the requirements and we were awarded our cycling honor.

Not long after that, a special Saturday evening program had been arranged, and the JMVs were responsible for the program. We did all sorts of things—showing how to tie various knots, some showing how to apply bandages and first aid to those who needed it. It was meant to explain to the church all the important things which we as JMVs had learned during our year as JMVs. One of the features of the program was a little dialogue which had been scripted for one of our close friends, Barrie Miller, and Uncle Russell and Daddy. The script was a very simple one. Barrie acted as a boy who was not a member of the JMVs and therefore had not learned all that Uncle Russell and Daddy had learned. In the script Barrie had a problem with his bike, and his wheel came off. It was then Uncle Russell and Daddy's responsibility to fix the problem because "we had our cycling honor." A bike was loaned for the occasion by one of the elders of the Hamilton church, Mr. Charlie Wilson. Barrie was to be so impressed with what we were able to do because of being in the JMVs that he was to ask if he could join the JMVs. It was a very simple and rather amateurish illustration of our "skills."

However, there was a most embarrassing finish to the story. When Brother Wilson was riding home on the bike, an incident occurred which could have been very dangerous. The wheel which we had so "expertly" put back onto the bike came off, and Brother Wilson had what proved to be a minor accident. It raised some question among the church members as to whether Uncle Russell and Daddy had justly earned their cycling honor. However, we were not stripped of our honor.

Associated with the JMV and the MV societies were the Annual Conference Junior and Senior camps. One had to be eight years old before he could attend a junior camp and sixteen years old to attend the senior camp. When we were eight years of age we wanted badly to go to the junior camp. We pled with Grandma, but Grandma thought we were too young. It was a long way to go from Newcastle to Port Macquarice where the camp was held. We cried when the train traveled past our home and we were not on it, for we were hoping to attend that camp; however, the camp was held nearer next year at a place called Green Point, on the ocean about 50 miles south of Newcastle. The next year Grandma sacrificed the money necessary to attend the week long camp.

The Youth Director of the conference was Pastor Wilfred Rudge, who was later to become a conference president. We liked him very much expect for one thing: he started dunking us under the water, and when he did it unexpectedly we swallowed some salt water which caused us to cough violently. The next year the camp was again held at Green Point, and again Grandma gave us the money to attend. Again we were put in the same unit, for they divided the children into units each of about six or seven youngsters. Uncle Russell was chosen as the leader of our unit. Every day the unit which had the most points from the day before had the honor of raising the Australian flag in the morning and lowering the flag in the evening. It was considered a great honor, and how strongly we wanted to win that honor!

Ours was a ragtag unit, but we worked very hard together. One of the important points was dealing with the tidiness of our tent and carefully making our beds in the morning. So we worked hard to clean the tent so that there was nothing for which to take points away from our unit. All the members of each unit were judged on whether they were ready on time for meetings and meals, and there were other ways the units could win points. However, halfway through the week we were delighted to be the unit to win for that day, and then on the final day of the camp our unit was again the unit chosen to raise and lower the flag. We felt very proud of that achievement. It would be right to say that none of us in the unit would have been very motivated to do all those things correctly except for the honor of raising the flag.

However, there was an incident at the camp which proved nasty. Apparently a couple of the boys who had been on duty helping peel potatoes and do other things in the kitchen had hollowed out a number of potatoes and put soap inside. They thought this would be a great joke. Those who got those potatoes had a very nasty experience. Of course it was not too hard to find out who were the boys which did it, for it was not a large group who were helping with the meal preparation. I have now forgotten what happened to those boys but we certainly found out that it was not considered funny by the counselors. That was the last time we were to attend junior camp because from the age of 12 we worked every school holiday, and that meant we could not go to camp. We believe the training we got from JMVs and our short time in MVs was a great blessing to our development in the Christian life.

> Train up a child in the way he should go: and when he is old, he will not depart from it. Proverbs 22:6

Family Photos

#1. Wedding of Colin and Russell's parents, Darcy and Hilda Standish [Sept. 1932]

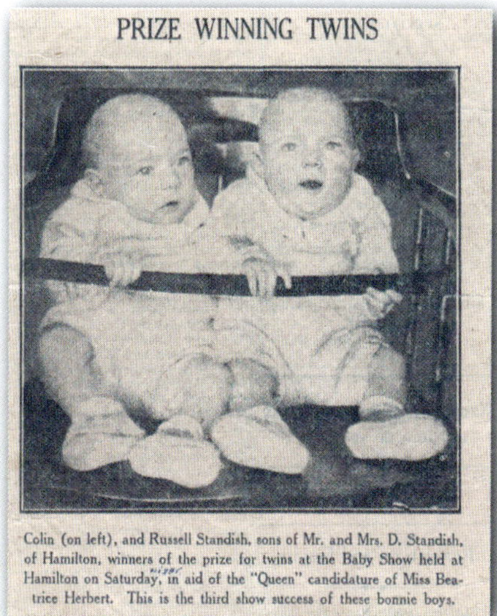

PRIZE WINNING TWINS

Colin (on left), and Russell Standish, sons of Mr. and Mrs. D. Standish, of Hamilton, winners of the prize for twins at the Baby Show held at Hamilton on Saturday, in aid of the "Queen" candidature of Miss Beatrice Herbert. This is the third show success of these bonnie boys.

#2. Colin & Russell, baby contest winners—*Newcastle Morning Herald* [May 1934]

#3. Colin and Russell, at 1 year and 10 months, in the first twin stroller purchased in the city of Newcastle [1935]

#4. Colin and Russell [July 1936]

Family Photos

#5. Colin and Russell with their great-grandfather, Samuel David Standish [Dec. 1936]

#7. Colin, Russell, and other students of Hamilton SDA High School. Robert Parr, principal, standing (L) [c 1945]

#6. Colin and Russell wearing school uniforms [c 1943]

#8. Colin, Delma (sister), and Russell Standish (1949)

Family Photos

#9. Colin (next to teacher in rear) in Dr. Geoffrey Rosenhain's education class [1951]

#12. Colin teaching at Ophir Glen, Northern NSW [1952]

#10. Colin and Russell (middle, second row), with the other teacher graduates from Avondale [1951]

#13. Delma, Darcy, E. I. Standish, Lyndon, Russell, Colin, Cheryl, and Hilda Standish—at Colin and Cheryl's wedding [1962]

#11. Colin, Lyndon, Hilda, Darcy, Delma, and Russell Standish [Dec. 1951]

Family Photos

#14. Colin and Cheryl Standish with Elder Wilcox dedicate Nigel (at 2.5 months) to the Lord [1983]

#17. Nigel, 14 months

#15. Timothy (son of Russell) with Colin and Cheryl at Nigel's dedication

#16. Nigel, 4 weeks

#18. Nigel with his grandma on his second birthday

Family Photos

#19. Father & son

#20. Father & son

#21. Grandma Bashen with her only two grandchildren

#22. Nigel loved his bikes

Family Photos

#23. Alexandra with
proud mother Cheryl [1985]

#25. Early family photo

#24. Alexandra a few months old

#26. Alexandra at dedication to the Lord
with New Zealand Pastor George Burnside
[Dec 1986]

Family Photos

#27. Nigel and Alexandra [1986]

#29. Nigel and Alexandra [1987]

#28. Nigel and Alexandra [1987]

#30. Nigel, 5 years old,
after he had lost his upper front teeth

Family Photos

#31. Nigel, 5 years old,
and Alexandra, 2 years old

#33. Alexandra, on the dog at the
Hartland formal garden [c 1987]

#32. Nigel, 6-year-old horseman

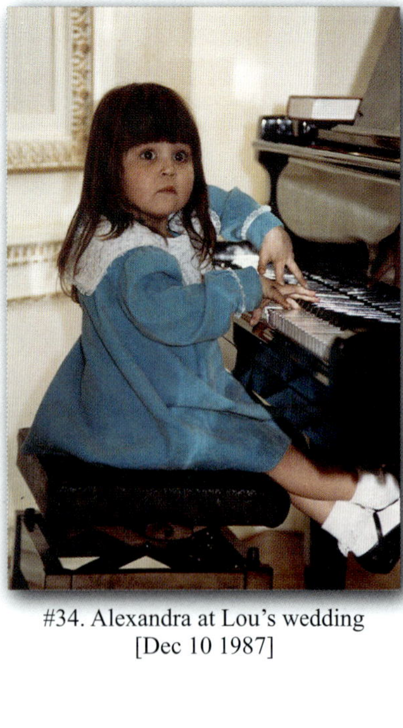

#34. Alexandra at Lou's wedding
[Dec 10 1987]

Family Photos

#35. When Father and Mother shared their 25th wedding anniversary at Hartland with Dr. and Mrs. Warren Peters [1988]

#37. Alexandra, about 3 years old

#36. Alexandra, the happy singer, 4 years old

#38. Nigel and Alexandra

Family Photos

#39. Family worship

#41. Nigel and Alexandra pet a wallaby on a visit to Australia

#40. Special occasion

#42. Nigel and Alexandra [1990]

Family Photos

#43. The elementary school [c 1992]

#45. Alexandra with her flowers

#44. Nigel loved to ride bikes
(about 7 years old)

#46. Alexandra growing up

Family Photos

#47. Elementary school students (Nigel in red; Alexandra, front row, right) with teacher

#49. Nigel, the pianist

#48. Family photo

#50. Nigel's graduation with fellow graduate, Randa Ellis [1996]

Family Photos

#51. Nigel, giving his elementary graduation address [1996]

#53. Hartland Academy students (Nigel, back row, second from left) [1999]

#52. Alexandra's baptism [1997]

#54. Alexandra becomes a teenager

Family Photos

#55. Feeding kangaroo in Australia

#57. Proclamation Singers
(Nigel, sixth from right)

#56. Alexandra, Nigel,
Cheryl, and Colin Standish

#58. Family photo at time of
Alexandra's academy graduation

Family Photos

#59. Nigel, preaching in Fortaleza, Brazil

#60. Academy graduation of Alexandra (right)
with Giancalo Perozo and Sandra Correa [2003]

#61. Nigel, preaching in the Hartland chapel

Family Photos

#62. Nigel, witnessing in South Korea

#64. Alexandra, Cheryl, and Nigel Standish

#63. Nigel, Cheryl, Colin,
and Alexandra Standish [2004]

#65. Alexandra Standish [2007]

Chapter 24

The End of the Second World War

Uncle Russell and Daddy were approaching their twelfth birthday. Frequently we heard that soon the Second World War would be over. The Allies (which included the United States, the Soviet Union, Great Britain, Australia, New Zealand, and other powers fighting on the same side) were being victorious over the Axis Powers (which included Germany, Japan, Austria, Hungary, Italy, and other powers). All the news reports said that the Allies were pushing back the Germans and then later the Japanese. There was great relief around Australia when this news was broadcast. However, it took longer than expected to secure the surrender of the Axis Powers. Both Germany and Japan wanted to negotiate conditions of their surrender. The Allies would accept only unconditional surrender. Reports began to surface that some of the German leaders had committed suicide, including Adolph Hitler, the dictator of Germany, and Himmler, the head of the dreaded SS (Secret Service), who were responsible for huge numbers losing their lives. Allied forces advanced toward Germany from every side. The Soviets came from the east, the British, French, and Americans came from the north, south, and west. Admiral Doinetz had taken over the leadership of Germany after the suicide of Hitler, but his rule was very brief, and soon the surrender in Europe was complete. At last, there was peace in Europe and North Africa.

However, the Japanese were still fighting. It was at this time that President Harry Truman, of the United States, made one of the most agonized decisions which any leader could make, and that was to allow an atomic bomb to be dropped on the city of Hiroshima. The bomb was dropped with a parachute which was meant to slow the decent of the bomb so the war plane which was carrying the bomb could travel far away before it exploded with its deadly radiation power. At least 25,000 people were killed. Many others were burned by radiation, and many of those later contracted cancer and other diseases and died premature deaths. This was devastating to the Japanese who now were in the most difficult position of deciding what to do. The Americans allowed word to filter to the Japanese emperor that they were planning to drop such a device on Tokyo near where the palace of Emperor Hirohito was located. However, the next bomb was dropped on Nagasaki with similar devastating results. Even though today those bombs would be considered small compared with what the present nuclear bombs could accomplish, that was more than enough at that point to secure the Japanese surrender.

Word of Japan's surrender soon reached the newspaper offices, the radio outlets and other communication agencies, and there was joy, great joy. We were told that when the war concluded bells would be rung all around the city, and there would be a school holiday. When we heard the bells pealing out across the city as we were walking to school that morning, we knew the war had ended, and, as all boys might be expected to do, Daddy and Uncle Russell were rejoicing that there was going to be a holiday. We continued to school to confirm that school was closed that day—as were most of the work places—and we made our way home.

Soon the radio stations were announcing that there would be a very special celebration that night in the Newcastle sportsground. We urged Grandpa to take us, which he did. Soon no traffic could travel up Hunter Street, the main street of Newcastle. Tens of thousands of civilians and soldiers alike crowded into the streets, and soon the streets were filled with many dancing the maypole as the ecstasy of the end of the war was beginning to be realized. There was great celebration and fireworks and spontaneous celebrations. It was certainly a wonderful and exciting time, but no one was counting the difficulties ahead in the post-war era of reconstruction. Australia itself had not been seriously hurt except in a few isolated places such as Darwin in the far north; nevertheless, there were great needs in other countries, especially in Great Britain, where food and clothes were in short supply. For many years Australian individuals, businesses, and government agencies all contributed to send "care packages" to Britain by the tens of thousands.

Much destruction had taken place in the cities of England by the terrible B1 and B2 bombs from Germany. The Germans would calculate as precisely as possible the amount of fuel necessary for these crude missiles to reach certain locations, knowing that once the fuel was used up the bomb would drop, hopefully on its target. Unfortunately it was not a precise science, and therefore not a few people lost their lives when the bombs dropped on domestic settlements instead of the industrial buildings. It was common for the warning sirens to sound in London and other cities, and people hastened to the air raid shelters, hoping they would have protection there.

Of course, much of the rest of Europe was devastated by the war. Only countries such as Switzerland and Sweden, which had remained neutral in the war, escaped the devastation. It did not matter which side of the war they were on, each country suffered terribly. The Germans suffered more than any nation, and the Italians, Austrians, Hungarians and other countries which had fought with the Axis Powers also suffered many casualties.

Already in the early part of the war countries such as France, Belgium, the Netherlands, Poland, and Czechoslovakia had been terribly ravaged. It was to take many years for the results of the war to fade. As is often the case, the countries were rejuvenated, destroyed buildings were rebuilt, and today there are few evidences of the terrible destruction which took place in that war. America helped greatly. The plan devised by General Marshall, known as the Marshall Plan, sent hundreds of millions of dollars in aid to the stricken nations, especially to countries like Germany. This helped in the rebuilding. Germany was divided into four parts after its defeat by the Allied Powers: the Russians took over the eastern part which they incorporated in the Warsaw Pact of communist Nations of Eastern Europe. The north, south, and west parts of Germany were divided between Britain, the United States, and France. However, after some years the portion of Germany governed by France,

Britain, and the United States was unified into what became known as West Germany. Germany successfully prospered and again became a powerful nation. Japan also rejuvenated quickly, and it became one of the most successful industrialized nations of the world. All this demonstrates the futility of war. Myriads lose their lives for that which years later is almost forgotten, and when a new generation arises they think little of the times past. So much of this war had been a part of our young lives—from five to twelve years of age—that Uncle Russell and Daddy could not imagine that there was any need for radio news bulletins after the war ended. Daddy asked Grandpa, "Is there any news on the radio now that the war is over?" Grandpa assured Daddy that the news would continue, and, of course, that it did.

Soon after the war ended came the terrible trials of leaders of various countries who had committed very serious war crimes. We were especially riveted upon the trial of German leaders at Nuremberg in West Germany. We followed them eagerly in the newspaper. Some of the leaders were sentenced to be hanged; some to greater or lesser prison terms. At least one, Goering, the head of the air force, committed suicide, with a small vial of cyanide which he had concealed the night before he was to be hanged.

War is a terrible thing. No wonder Sister White wrote,

> Through spiritualism, Satan appears as a benefactor of the race, healing the diseases of the people, and professing to present a new and more exalted system of religious faith; but at the same time he works as a destroyer. His temptations are leading multitudes to ruin. Intemperance dethrones reason; sensual indulgence, strife, and bloodshed follow. Satan delights in war, for it excites the worst passions of the soul and then sweeps into eternity its victims steeped in vice and blood. It is his object to incite the nations to war against one another, for he can thus divert the minds of the people from the work of preparation to stand in the day of God. *The Great Controversy,* p. 589

We must remember that before Jesus returns there will be increasing incidents of war. Only God can give us peace in our hearts now.

> And ye shall hear of wars and rumours of wars: see that ye be not troubled: for all these things must come to pass, but the end is not yet. Matthew 24:6

> Great peace have they which love thy law: and nothing shall offend them. Psalm 119:165

Chapter 25

Running Away From Home

At the age of eight Uncle Russell and Daddy began to show an interest in saving postage stamps from other countries. We were fascinated by what were on the stamps of the different countries. It was to develop in Uncle Russell and Daddy a lifelong interest in geography. As we found a stamp from a new country we would look it up in the atlas and then learn the capital of that country. Of course, we did not find stamps from every country in the world; however, we took up the challenge to learn the capital of every country in the world. The world map has changed much since then, and the names of many countries have changed, the borders of countries have changed, new countries have been established, old countries have been merged into other countries, and some have new names for their capitals. We had a wonderful time learning so much geography. Our stamp collection steadily increased, and we would spend time attaching the stamps we received in our stamp album.

We had been collecting for four years when an incident occurred which led Uncle Russell and Daddy to run away from home. We often worked on the stamps on Sunday and left our stamp album and stamps and other things untidily around the house. Grandma had warned us numbers of times that if we continued to do that she would burn the stamp album. We, of course, did not believe that she would do such a drastic thing. However, one Sunday afternoon we asked where our stamp album had gone, and Grandma said, "I warned you, and I have burned it." We were shocked and filled with great anger. We talked together and we decided that we were going to run away from home. Uncle Russell insisted that we leave a note in the letterbox so that our parents would find it the next morning telling them that we had run away from home.

When we left, we walked down Dumaresq Street until we came to Beaumont Street where we turned right and then crossed Everton Street, Veda Street, Denison Street, Tudor Street, James Street, Lindsay Street, and Donald Street until we came to the Hamilton railway station. When no one was looking we crossed over onto the tracks, deciding that we would walk the 600 miles to Brisbane following the railway line. We had no money, and we had no warm clothes with us. It certainly was an impulsive and foolish decision. As we walked north toward the next railway station at Waratah, we saw thunder clouds rising in the sky. Maybe this was the providence of God. We realized we had no raincoat and it looked as if it would be a very serious storm. We began to wonder whether we really wanted to leave home and go to another location. Eventually, we decided in spite of what Grandma had done, it would be better to go home.

We retraced our steps until we came to our home, opened the gate, and took the note out of the box. Not until we were grown up did we tell Grandma and Grandpa that we had tried to run away from home. We certainly were happy to be home in our house when the rain began to fall. It is so important for children to realize how wonderful home is. We never again thought of leaving home. Had we learned the lesson to obey our parents, this situation would have never happened.

> Children, obey your parents in all things: for this is well pleasing unto the Lord. Colossians 3:20

Chapter 26

The Best Night of the Week

When Uncle Russell and Daddy were little boys, the best night of the week was Friday night. We loved Friday night, and there were many good reasons that Friday night was our favorite night. When we were three to ten years of age, Grandpa worked on the railways, and he would come home every Friday afternoon for the weekend.

There is something else which was special about Friday night. We can never remember getting a spanking on Friday night. That was not true of other nights of the week. Friday night was special at tea (supper) time. Every Friday afternoon mother made soup. It was made either with split peas and vegetables or with barley and vegetables, and our mother always made it rich in vegetables, and it tasted so good. She would put celery, carrots, parsnips, swede (rutabagas), potato and onion. It did not matter whether it was winter, spring, summer or autumn—we always had soup Friday night, and to follow it our mother always had a special bun for us.

There were other things which also made Friday night so very special. We knew we had to hurry straight home from school to do our chores. Often we helped mother cut up the vegetables for the soup. In those days we knew nothing about frozen vegetables or supermarkets. Once or twice a week the fruit and vegetable man (the "green grocer") would come with his horse and open cart, stop at our front gate, and Grandma would buy whatever fruit and vegetables she felt the family needed for the week. The green grocer had for sale bunches of mixed vegetables, tied together by their tops, ready to be made into soup. Our job was to peel the vegetables, then cut them into dices to the size which mother desired. Then we carried the leftover scraps down the backyard to throw over the pen for the fowls to eat.

When, at the age of nine, we moved to the Newcastle suburb of Hamilton, it was much easier because three blocks from where we lived there was a fruit and vegetable shop where we could purchase whatever we needed for the family supplies. Sometimes we were given the shopping list by Grandma, and we would buy and take the fruits and vegetables back home.

It was also easier to have our baths because we now had a "copper" (a large copper boiling pot) in the laundry room of 78 Dumaresq Street where we lived. The copper was filled with water for our baths and heated by a wood fire. It was one of our jobs to gather the wood and light the fire for our Friday afternoon baths. We had Great-grandpa and bachelor Great-uncle Ol living with us. Once Grandpa joined the Sanitarium Health Food Company, we always had plenty of wood. Grandpa would bring home wooden boxes and some cardboard boxes, and we would always have a pile of wood. It was our responsibility to break up the boxes which would be used to heat the water which we would run into the copper from the tap above it.

Then, one at a time, the family members would have a bath. Usually Uncle Russell and Daddy would bathe first. The first one to bathe would bucket the boiling water out of the copper into the bathtub, where cold water was run into the bath from the tap. While the first one of us was bathing, the other one was carrying out the responsibility of feeding the "chooks" (chickens). Usually this was fairly easy in the afternoon because it was a matter of throwing them a suitable quantity of wheat. Sometimes, we would need to also refill the water trough for the chooks, especially in the hot weather.

As soon as our baths were taken we would dress in our pajamas. In the winter we wore warm woolen pajamas, for we had no central heating, and rarely did we have any other form of heating. In the summer it would be lighter cotton pajamas. We learned the importance of conserving water, for the second one of us would likely add some more hot water into the water in which the first one had bathed. We would also fill the copper up again, making sure there was plenty of fire to reach the boil so that we could be followed first by Grandma and finally by Grandpa until all the baths were taken. Even in the summer when the sun was still high in the sky Grandpa, Uncle Russell and Daddy would dress in our pajamas, and Grandma in her nightgown. Usually father and mother had a dressing gown around them, especially in the wintertime.

The season of the year—summer or wintertime—determined whether we ate before or after having opened the Sabbath. How we enjoyed the opening of Sabbath! We were all freshly bathed, and Grandma would play the piano as we all sang, each one taking a turn in choosing a favorite hymn. Finally, Grandpa would decide it was time to pray, and it would usually be just before the sun set as he invited the Holy Spirit into the family and asked the blessings of God upon the keeping of the Sabbath day. Then, Grandpa would read an extensive passage from the Spirit of Prophecy. Many times it was from the *Testimonies for the Church*.

Today, most people would believe that the *Testimonies* are too heavy for boys who have not yet reached their teenage years, but some of it was very interesting to us. It was there that Uncle Russell and Daddy learned much about the life of Sister White. We learned about the story of Hannah More and the way she had been so ignored by the people at Battle Creek. (See *Testimonies*, vol. 1, p. 666.)

We also learned about God's stand in time of war, that we were not to participate in warfare. This was, indeed, very important because for some of this time it was part of the Second World War years. When Uncle Russell and Daddy were growing up toward our teen years, Grandpa and Grandma wanted them to understand that it was not God's purpose that we take part in war.

There were many other interesting experiences, especially in the early *Testimonies*. There was counsel and instruction to individual people or groups of people. Neither Uncle Russell nor Daddy understood it all well, nor did we always appreciate the length of the passages which Grandpa read, but they were a wonderful foundation for our knowledge as we were growing up to understand some of the saving principles which God had given to us.

If we had eaten before the setting of the sun, after worship we often sang more hymns, and then we were free to take out our books as we grew older and read whatever we desired to read. Grandma had given these books to us for birthday and Christmas as gifts. Often they were missionary books; other times they were nature books. How we enjoyed learning from these books! At the same time Grandpa and Grandma would quietly read other important devotional books.

I guess that is where Uncle Russell and Daddy began to develop an interest in serving in the mission field. We were so inspired by the mission stories about Africa, China, India, the South Pacific, South America and other parts of the world. In the end, Uncle Russell spent about twenty years in mission service in Southeast Asia, as well as serving in England. Daddy spent much less time in mission service, only serving in Jamaica for a little more than three years, but we greatly enjoyed our experience.

Since we have been in self-supporting work, we have gone to many countries of the world to teach and to preach the gospel of Jesus, both to Seventh-day Adventists and to those not of our faith. We have seen many souls led to God's church and to the wonderful three angels' messages. Both of us now have been in more than 100 different countries of the world in a response to the words of Jesus in Matthew 28:19, 20:

> Go ye therefore, and teach all nations, baptizing them in the name of the Father, and of the Son, and of the Holy Ghost: teaching them to observe all things whatsoever I have commanded you: and, lo, I am with you always, even unto the end of the world. Amen.

Friday night was such a special night and we always had the privilege of going to bed relatively early. We also had the luxury of getting up a little later, although not too much later, on Sabbath morning because Grandpa and Grandma always taught us to be punctual, and that meant being at Sabbath school well before it started. Usually we would begin our approximate ten minute walk to church at about 9:00 A.M. so we could be there at least by a quarter after nine. In those days, Sabbath school started at 9:45 A.M., so the Standish family was there well before most other attendees, although in those times almost all people were at Sabbath school before the starting time.

While we did not completely understand the significance of God's Word in those days, there is no question that Grandpa and Grandma were following the instructions which Moses gave after presenting the Ten Commandments in Deuteronomy, chapter 5:

> Hear, O Israel: The Lord our God is one Lord: And thou shalt love the Lord thy God with all thine heart, and with all thy soul, and with all thy might. And these words, which I command thee this day, shall be in thine heart: And thou shalt teach them diligently unto thy children, and shalt talk of them when thou sittest in thine house, and when thou walkest by the way, and when thou liest down, and when thou risest up. And thou shalt bind them for a sign upon thine hand, and they shall be as frontlets between thine eyes. And thou shalt write them upon the posts of thy house, and on thy gates. Deuteronomy 6:4–9

Chapter 27

Working on our Holidays

As you know, Grandpa did not receive a big salary, for low salaries were common at that time. As Uncle Russell and Daddy were getting older, the cost of clothes and our education in the Seventh-day Adventist school kept increasing, and Mother decided that we should do whatever we could to help provide funds for our clothes and for our education at school—not only for the fees but for text books and other supplies which are necessary in education. Grandma suggested to Grandpa that he see if there might be some work which Uncle Russell and Daddy could do at the Sanitarium Health Food Company warehouse where Grandpa worked. He talked to the manager, and the manager said that they needed someone to wash jars for the honey, for one of the big sellers for the Sanitarium was their high-quality honey. As Grandpa was in charge of the warehouse, he became a specialist in purchasing in big quantities the best quality honey in Australia.

In Australia it was generally acknowledged that the yellow box honey was the best honey in the country. The yellow box was a variety of the flowering eucalyptus tree which grew in dryer parts of Australia. It was a very light-colored honey with a very smooth texture. Most families at this time were able to buy small refrigerators, and they would put the honey in the refrigerator and that would stiffen it up. Grandpa would buy nothing but the best honey, and it was necessary to have all the jars in which to pour the honey to be sparkling clean. So our first job was to wash thousands of honey jars by hand. This was a heavy responsibility for two twelve year -old lads because if we did not do the job very carefully then we would soon lose our job. Of course Grandpa was there to make sure that we did it thoroughly and that we did our best.

It was very monotonous work, and the days were long, for in those days we worked 44 hours a week. We did the best we could. Grandpa and Grandma had made it very plain to us that any work which we did, we had to do it well. We received one pound and ten shillings (three dollars) each week for this work. Yet, in those days, that was a good help to our parents in buying food for us and building up enough money to pay our school fees, buy our school supplies, and sometimes help to buy us clothes as we were then growing rapidly. From this first work experience, in the shorter holidays, the autumn and the spring, we would find short term jobs. This included working with the Sanitarium Health Food Company, accompanying the men who traveled from store to store selling the various products which the Sanitarium Health Food Company manufactured.

In those days most people did not own cars, and therefore they needed stores within easy access. Instead of supermarkets, there were many small stores scattered around the towns and countryside. These stores would order breakfast foods, honey, marmite and many other products which were produced by the Sanitarium Health Food Company. When we worked as side boys on a delivery van, it was our responsibility to haul from the truck into the store whatever goods they had ordered. Sometimes we worked with Grandpa when he became a traveler (salesman) for the Sanitarium Health Food Company. He had not learned to drive until then, well into his 30s. It would be many more years before Grandpa would own a car.

There were times we worked as side boys for a cordial (soft-drink) factory—a small factory operated by a Seventh-day Adventist whose son was a little older than we were and attended the Newcastle Seventh-day Adventist high school at the time we did. The cordial factory did not sell to stores, but had built up quite a cliental to whom they delivered their cordials to the homes. It was our responsibility to get the cordials into the homes. This was work which we did during the short breaks.

In Australia, our summer break was over the Christmas and New Year period, from about the middle of December to the end of January. One summer break, we worked for the largest home building company in the city of Newcastle as builders' laborers. Most summers, however, we spent picking and bagging potatoes which had been either dug by horse and plow or by a tractor pulling a piece of equipment called a potato digger. Truly that was hard work. We had to leave home very early in the morning, walk about a mile to the Hamilton railway station, go about twenty miles north on a train, change trains at East Maitland, and then travel another three or four miles on a little train which traveled back and forth between East Maitland and the town of Morpeth, stopping at three stations along the way. Then we would walk to the farm where we to pick potatoes. For one farm, we had to cross the Hunter River in a little boat to get to the farm. This was in the boiling, humid heat of the summer, but it was profitable for us. For each large sack of potatoes which we picked, we were paid two shillings and sixpence (25 cents) if dug by the mechanical potato digger, or three shillings (30 cents) if dug by the horse and plow. We received more for the latter because the potato digger left the potatoes on top of the ground and thus they were easier to pick.

We proved to be among the very fastest pickers of potatoes on these farms. We had to be careful because we had to grade the potatoes between the "chats" (which weighed less than two ounces), and the regular potatoes. If the grading was done poorly, the farmer would tell the one responsible to open the bags and sort them out again. Therefore, they were very particular about the potato pickers. Uncle Russell and Daddy very quickly won the confidence of the farmers, and we were in great demand in the region which grew large quantities of potatoes.

Daddy remembers on one occasion we asked the farmer we were working with to keep what he was to pay us until, between the two of us, we had earned more than ten pounds (twenty dollars). He agreed to do this. Only once in our lives had we seen a ten-pound note. We knew it was red in color, and we wanted to own one ourselves, at least for a short time, and show it to our parents. We were very familiar with the five-pound note which was blue, but the ten-pound note was the highest note in the Australian currency at that time. The farmer agreed, and he eventually gave us a check for more than ten pounds, which represented at least 80 bags of potatoes which we had picked. We went to the bank in Morpeth and asked if they had a ten pound note. To our great joy they did, and we received that with the rest of the money which was due to us. How proud we were to display it to our parents!

We remember that we had invited one of our friends who was younger than us to come with us if he wanted to make some money. He did so, but for two days he made terrible mistakes in his grading, so the owner of the farm came to us and told us he wanted *us* back, but he did not want our friend Geof to come back. Geof left God's church and later married and had a young family. However, he died in his early 30s from cancer. Daddy visited him at the hospital in the outer district of Belmont. Daddy urged him to re-commit his life to the Lord, but he made the tragic response, "It's too late; I made the wrong decision." How tragic!

Another summer we cut millet which was used for bird seed and the straw for making brooms. There was a small group of workers in the team. At first we would fold the millet stalks over, at about waist high, one row one way and the next row across the other way to make what was called a "table." Then, with a sharp knife we would cut the stalk ends with the straw and seeds, and after cutting a bundle we would put it on the top of the "table," which was made by the two rows which had been folded over each other. Later someone would gather up the bundles and prepare them to be hauled away by trucks.

The two leaders of this team were aborigines. It was one of the first times we had the opportunity to talk with aborigines. They were nice men, but they were very concerned about how difficult it was for their children in white-dominated schools. It seemed that the white children picked on them and ridiculed them. How sad! We felt sorry for them as boys. We even remember Grandpa coming up for a few days and doing some millet cutting with us. This work, besides the chores we did at home, was very good training for Uncle Russell and Daddy. While unfortunately we did not learn any specific skills, nevertheless we did learn how to work well and effectively. Uncle Russell and Daddy believe it is good for all young people to learn how to work well, to be responsible, honest and productive. However, it is also good for all young people to learn a special practical skill. The Bible commands the training of young people to work well.

> Slothfulness casteth into a deep sleep; and an idle soul shall suffer hunger. Proverbs 19:15

Chapter 28

Vacationing in South Australia

Grandpa was born June 22, 1912, in a little village in South Australia called Vine Vale in Kabunga Cottage, a tiny four-room house in which members of our family lived for 90 years from 1884 to the death of Great-great-uncle Oscar in 1974. Because it was a German community, he grew up speaking German until he went to school at the age of seven. He was the first generation of children in the Barossa Valley who were educated in the English language. That had been a requirement of the government after the First World War where some of the German speaking Australian citizens were suspected of having sympathies for, if not helping, the German side. Our family had no problems because we had an English name, the result of your Great-great-great-grandfather Thomas Standish, marrying a German woman, Anna Elizabeth Heider. Each generation married into German families but the Standish name remained. You see, almost all the people who lived in the Barossa Valley were German immigrants or their descendants.

Most of the family had become Seventh-day Adventists in 1915 when a lay evangelist, Brother Bachaus led quite a few of the Lutheran families to the Seventh-day Adventist faith. Great-great-grandfather Samuel Standish was one of them.

When Grandfather was sixteen years old, he traveled to Avondale College to prepare for the ministry and was there for more than three years, but he did not finish the ministerial course. Years later, Grandpa became a worker for the New South Wales Government Railway when

Uncle Russell and Daddy were three years old. Because he was a worker on the railway, the New South Wales Government Railways paid for the whole family to travel free of charge anywhere in the state of New South Wales. This gave a wonderful opportunity for the whole family to visit Grandpa's relatives every Christmas. That meant that we could either go to South Australia via Melbourne or via Broken Hill which was a silver, lead and zinc mining city about 700 miles west of Sydney and located close to the state of South Australia. We did not travel on the inter-city express from Newcastle to Sydney because that would have cost us one shilling and sixpence (fifteen cents) each for a special reservation on that train, and our parents were very careful not to spend money on "luxuries." Therefore we traveled on the slow train, often stopping at all stations, and thus instead of taking two hours and eighteen minutes, it would take well over four hours to reach Sydney from Newcastle where we lived.

At Sydney Central Railway Station we would catch the Forbes mail train. This was a train which carried mail as well as passengers west to the town of Forbes and other towns on the way. Not far away from Forbes was another town, Parkes. Early in the morning the train would arrive at Parkes, where we would change trains for what was called the Silver City Express, which traveled more than 400 miles between Parkes and the silver mining city of Broken Hill. The Silver City Express would cover the distance in not much more than eight hours—very fast for those times. The western plains of New South Wales are very flat, and we would pass through desert areas so different from anything with which we were familiar. The train was a rail motor—that is, instead of depending upon the conventional steam engines of the day, it had a small diesel engine in the first carriage. Somehow we enjoyed this trip. It would stop at a few small towns including Ivanhoe and Menindee. Well we remember on one occasion when the train broke down in a desert area, and we had to wait for hours before the train could resume its journey to Broken Hill.

At Broken Hill we usually hired a taxi, something my parents hated to do, but it was about a three-quarters of a mile journey between the terminus of the Silver City Express operated by the New South Wales State

Government Railways and the privately owned, three-foot-six-inch (a little more than a meter) gauged Silverton Railway, a conventional steam engine train which traveled from Broken Hill through Peterborough to Terowie. It was very unusual to have a private train in Australia, for most of the trains were operated by the state governments. Because it was on a narrow gauge the train rocked much more than the trains we were used to on the four-foot eight-and-one-half-inch (about one and one-half meters) gauges of the New South Wales state railway.

On one occasion we had a very uncertain journey. During the war, ordinary citizens were forbidden to leave the state in which they lived. The only way citizens could obtain permission to travel interstate was if one of their parents was 70 years of age or older or if a doctor certified that a parent was very sick or a child in another state was very sick. As Great-grandma Standish was still in her 50s at this time, Grandpa could not get permission. So Grandpa decided that the family should go in the hope that using the private railway it may be possible to cross into South Australia without being stopped. This was too much uncertainty for Grandma and she refused to go. However, Uncle Russell and Daddy were ready for such an adventure, so we accompanied Grandpa.

We could tell that Grandpa was very nervous when we came to Broken Hill. We caught the taxi, and since he was so nervous, Grandpa left his Gladstone bag in the taxi. However, the taxi driver was very kind, and when he discovered it he came back and found Grandpa and gave it to him. Now Grandpa had to go to the ticket counter and see if he could purchase tickets from Broken Hill to Adelaide. We were with Grandpa when he went to the counter, and how nervous he was! He said, "One and two halves to Adelaide," meaning one adult and two children. He forgot to say "and return." But calmly the man at the ticket counter asked "Single or return?" A very flustered Grandpa said, "Oh, return." And we did get to South Australia. Everyone knew that Broken Hill was a frontier town, as so many mining towns are, and that the miners took their vacations in Adelaide rather than in Sydney because it was only about half as far to Adelaide as it was to Sydney, the capital of New South Wales. Therefore it would seem that the government turned a blind eye to these miners going off to Adelaide across the South Australian border.

On another occasion during the Second World War, we were on a huge train of more than twenty carriages, filled with many soldiers obviously traveling to special destinations. Unfortunately some of the soldiers became drunk, and one of them walked back to the toilet, but someone else was occupying it. After a little while, when his banging on the door did not succeed in getting into the toilet, he suddenly punched his fist through the opaque glass at the upper part of the door and very seriously injured his hand, resulting in much bleeding. The train officials had to take him off the train at the next station so that he could obtain medical care.

On another occasion coming back from Adelaide, we had already reached Parkes and had changed onto the Forbes mail train to travel to Sydney. On the train was a little Australian in our eight person compartment as well as a big professional Russian wrestler. The little Australian had much alcohol to drink, and he began to boast to the good-natured Russian wrestler. It was comical but sad to see this drunken man challenge the Russian wrestler to a fight. The Russian wrestler was very patient with him and just smiled. The same man, when the train made a lengthy stop at a railway station for refreshments, purchased a cup of tea. Before he had finished drinking it, the train started to move out of the station. He saw a porter and called out to him and threw the cup to him and, of course, the contents splashed all over the poor porter as he tried to catch the cup. These were very strange experiences for little boys from a Christian home.

Now a little about our stay in South Australia with Great-grandma Standish and Great-great-uncle Oscar, who was a bachelor. We loved to go across even though it was very hot in the summer. That region of Australia has what is called a Mediterranean climate, where the rain falls during the winter time and almost none falls in the summer. Therefore the conservation of water was very important, and most of the time people had only one storage tank, or at most two tanks, to store water during the winter time to provide for every water need that they had throughout the summer months. We had always been warned to be careful with water. One day however, Uncle Russell and Daddy were playing when somehow we poked a stick through the water tank and the water started to leak out. We were very afraid that Great-great-uncle Oscar would be very angry with us. Certainly Grandma was very upset as one of us held back the water with his hand over the hole while the other went to report what had taken place. Providentially, Great-great-uncle Oscar was a very practical man and he soon had repaired the hole, but not before we had a very strong tongue-lashing from Grandma. Great-great-uncle Oscar was very kind to us in the situation.

We loved to run through the vineyards; although, because we did not wear shoes except for church or on special occasions, our feet often burned on the hot, sandy soil. However, we loved the fruit. Yes, most of the acreage in that large valley was used for the wine industry. Very sad!

On the other hand, it grew the most luscious stone fruit. We especially remember the very large, sweet apricots. It also provided excellent almonds and walnuts, again very much larger than we had seen elsewhere. Lining the front fence was a long row of olive trees, and Italian people came to harvest the olives every year. However, Great-great-uncle Oscar always picked a large amount of olives and cured them himself to last for the year. We really enjoyed them.

There was no electricity in the home; their floor was cement right on top of the dirt. We were intrigued when Grandpa said to us, "We've got to go to bury the pig." We wondered what pig had died, because there were no pigs near Great-grandma's home, but that was their way of saying that they were filling in that toilet hole with dirt after digging another pit toilet. Everything seemed so old-fashioned, even in those days when we had so little in our home back in New South Wales. It seemed that we lived in a palace compared with the way Great-grandma lived. Yet, she was always happy and hard working. Twice a week she would walk the five miles into the town of Angaston to hand wash the clothes of some of the more wealthy people, and then she would walk back home; yet never did we hear her complain. We saw her making bread in the brick oven beside her wood stove. They always gathered and chopped up old stumps of grape vines for the fire.

It was a different experience going to the Nuriootpa church, a little Seventh-day Adventist church in the Barossa Valley. That church sent a large number of its boys to Avondale College to train for the ministry. Many of them became strong workers for the Lord—men such as Pastor Erwin Roenfelt, who became a division president in what was then called the Northern European Division and later an associate ministerial secretary of the General Conference. George Maywald became a departmental director both in the Southern Asian Division and the Australasian (South Pacific) Division; Bill Zeunet became a leader in the Sanitarium Health Food work. Pastor Alfred Kranz became principal of New Zealand Missionary College (Longburn) and West Australia Missionary College (Carmel), and later he was to become chairman of the Bible department at Avondale College, a position he held when we were students there. We had the opportunity to take his full year class in New Testament epistles, which was the only Bible class we took at Avondale College.

When we were boys, some of the members still came to church with their horses and buggies. At that time, almost all the services were held in English, which was a help to us. Not too long before, many of the services had been held in German. As Great-grandma had neither horse nor motor transportation, she would walk the five miles each way to the Nuriootpa church. That meant that as little boys, we walked to church and back. It was really a very great challenge for us to keep up with the pace that our little Great-grandmother walked as she went across the vineyards for that five-mile journey to church. However, Great-great-uncle Oscar had owned a Model A Ford pick-up truck which was broken down most of the times we visited, but once or twice it was actually in running condition. It was considered a luxury when we could go to church in that old Model A truck. Its motor was so weak that it could hardly get up even relatively small hills, but somehow it always managed to do so, even if some of us had to get out of the truck to lighten the load.

By the way, we never saw Great-grandmother Standish arrive late for Sabbath school. She was always there well before it started. When we consider today how so many people are late for Sabbath school, or never come at all, even though we have modern transportation, we marvel at the wonderful dedication of our forebears.

Another memorable experience in South Australia was meal time. Great-grandmother called us to the meals which were always ready at the same time every day. We would all stand around the table and there we would bow our heads as Great-great-uncle Oscar prayed. His prayer over the very simple food was very earnest and filled with thankfulness. It was not a meaningless prayer which he prayed—just the opposite. It was a very lengthy prayer. At the end of the meal we were anxious boys wanting to get away from the table and play. Yet, we dare not do that. We had to wait until everyone was finished, for meals were a very important social time. Many things were discussed at mealtime, and it took a long time for the last one—usually Great-great-uncle Oscar—to finish. It was Great-great-uncle Oscar who would give the signal, and we would stand again as he prayed thanking the Lord for the provision of our physical needs.

Worship time was always a special time—morning and evening. It was not a rushed few minutes. Great-great-uncle Oscar would always lead out. Normally he used the Martin Luther German Bible, but he would condescend to offer the worship with the use of the English King James Bible. Frequently, however, the worships were punctuated with Great-great-uncle Oscar saying, "But the Martin Luther Bible says. . . ." He always seemed to believe that the Martin Luther Bible was just a little more authentic than the English King James Bible.

Great-great-uncle Oscar was also fascinated with bees, and he always had two or three bee hives. We had the privilege of watching him rob the hives of honey and gather some honey comb. We also enjoyed the honey at our meals.

Across the vineyard lived Great-great-auntie Alvenie, usually called "Auntie Venie." She was a very kind and loving Great-great-aunt. However, she was married to a very rude man, Great-great-uncle Augustus Klix, who was not a Seventh-day Adventist. Whenever we visited Great-great-auntie Venie he would almost ignore us and Grandpa and Grandma would not enter into more than a one- or two-word conversation. Uncle Russell and Daddy were scared of him. Ironically, he raised pigs for an income. We somehow felt that he fitted in with these repulsive animals.

Great-great-uncle Oscar earned a little money picking stone fruit in season. However, he refused to pick grapes because they were used to make wine. He also made a little money repairing pans and kettles using solder and his soldering iron, which he heated over an open fire. He also repaired some watches and clocks, but he always said that he was not as clever as his father, Great-great-grandpa Samuel Standish.

The Standish family was well known for its interest in gold mining, in what were called the Adelaide hills behind where Great-grandma Standish lived. There had been some successful mining. Great-great-grandfather Samuel Standish, and his two sons, Great-great-uncle Fred and Great-great-uncle Oscar loved to go gold mining. They never did find much gold, but they had files with small, tiny pieces of gold in them, and once in a while they sold that gold to recover some finance. Once Uncle Russell and Daddy went up to the hills with Great-great-uncle Oscar and Great-great-uncle Fred. With much earnestness, Great-great-uncle Oscar pointed out how he believed the gold vein traveled through the hill. Yet they never did strike it rich. Great-great-uncle Oscar told us how, on one occasion many years before, they had dug down and given up; however, a couple of other young Germans dug just another two feet, and they came across sufficient gold to pay for their journey back to Germany to see the land of their forebears. That did not happen to the Standish family.

Perhaps above everything else, the trips to South Australia taught us how, in a simple environment, people who loved God with all their heart and soul served God so faithfully. It is much more difficult to have the same level of dedication in the prosperity of today's society. We cannot forget the Words of Jesus,

> It is easier for a camel to go through the eye of a needle, than for a rich man to enter into the kingdom of God. Matthew 19:24

Chapter 29

Sports

It was at the Seventh-day Adventist school that we learned a love for sports. This was very sad because it has been one of the greatest difficulties for Uncle Russell and Daddy to get away from the idolatry of sports. When we were pupils at Cardiff Public School, every Wednesday afternoon was a sports afternoon. We were not interested at all in sports. However, we were required to go down to the park and were assigned to a teacher in one sport or another. If the teacher was not watching us closely, we would sneak away to avoid taking part. We knew nothing about sports, therefore we had no skill in sports, and we wanted to avoid the embarrassment of not knowing how to play sports.

The time came that the school was looking to choose runners in the various age groups to take part in the Newcastle and regional sports carnival at the sports ground in the city of Newcastle. Children of each age were lined up, and races took place to decide who would represent the school in the various age divisions. At the time we were eight years of age, and we were raced against other eight-year-olds. Uncle Russell and Daddy were chosen to be part of the eight-year-old relay team. Daddy was chosen also to run in the sprint. Uncle Russell, unfortunately, had a boil behind one of his legs, and therefore he missed out on being chosen to be an individual runner. However, by the time all the many schools were gathered together, Uncle Russell's leg had healed, and our relay team came second out of all the relay teams. It was disappointing to us because there were three fast runners in our team but the third runner in the relay was considerably slower, and a number of teams caught up and passed him. It was only a tremendous burst of running by Uncle Russell as the fourth runner in the relay team that brought us back into second place.

I remember we were taken up before the whole assembly school and congratulated on our performance. This was one of the few times that we seemed to meet the approbation of Mr. Petterfield, the school principal. Because of our speed, we attracted the attention of the rugby league football coach. He sent a letter home to our mother asking permission for us to be trained for the school's football team. However, our mother wrote back a decided "No," and we were quite happy about it.

However, when we began to attend the Seventh-day Adventist school, our principal was very fond and quite competent in sports. The three sports which attracted him were cricket, tennis, and table tennis. He was part of a team of Seventh-day Adventists who played in the "A-grade" table tennis competition in Newcastle. He also was involved in some lower grade tennis tournaments, and he loved to play cricket. We admired him so much that we followed him and soon became very fascinated with sports. You do not have to guess which three sports we especially got involved with, although it was to expand to a number of other sports such as soccer, and occasionally even rugby.

When Uncle Russell and Daddy began playing these sports, they were about the poorest of any of the students. Mr. Parr put a table-tennis table in the school shed, and we both remember how the other students laughed at how difficult we found it to keep the ball on the other side of the table with the paddle. But that only made us determined to do better, and to our great surprise we found that in a short period of time of determined practice we were able to play as well, and soon better, than all the other students. The same thing happened with tennis and especially cricket. We soon realized we had great aptitude in sports, something we had never dreamed of before. Sadly, like all of Satan's worldly attractions, we became addicted, fiercely competitive, and determined to beat those with whom we played.

Daddy still remembers when he first beat Mr. Parr at table tennis. Of course, being an "A-grade" player in our city's competition, he was far better than any of the students or the other two male staff members, at least at the beginning. But it was always the goal of the students to see if they could beat him. At first no one came close to beating him. But as we practiced and matured, we were getting closer.

One class Daddy had finished his work early, so Mr. Parr said, "Come down and we will play a set of table tennis." As always, I was determined to do my best to beat him, with all the wrong, selfish motivations. Of course, Mr. Parr was very anxious to keep his undefeated record, although he realized that very rapidly his young students were improving and coming closer to his skill. I was fourteen years old at the time, and to my great shock and delight, by the narrowest of margins, I beat him in that set. You can imagine the excitement of Daddy when he was telling all the students that he had just beaten Mr. Parr. Of course, many of the students never did beat Mr. Parr, but it was not long after that that Uncle Russell beat him once. After we had beaten him once, it was a very rare occasion when he would beat us, and the time soon came when we were playing considerably better than he could play.

He then decided that we should challenge the Sanitarium Health Food Company team. Eight players were chosen, the three teachers and five students. They were divided into two teams—the first team and the second team. The first team was ranked: Daddy, first; Uncle Russell, second; Mr. Parr, third; and Mr. Winston Dunlop, fourth. The second team was ranked: Ron Swan, first; Doug Ling, second; Mr. Hill, third; and Bob Craig, fourth. To the surprise of the Sanitarium team, the school's second team defeated their second team eleven games to nine. However, the Sanitarium first team easily defeated the school's first team fourteen games to six. Daddy was the only one to win two out of his four singles matches. The other three each one won one, and Uncle Russell and Daddy won one of the doubles matches. But that only made us more determined, and there was a rematch some months later. In the rematch, the school team won both the first and the second contests—the first team by a narrow margin of eleven games to nine, and the second team by a margin of twelve games to eight. We were now hooked on sports like a drug addict. Cricket became our favorite sport; however, with both Uncle Russell and Daddy quickly becoming the best cricket players in the school, both at bowling and batting.

While we were only fourteen years of age, one day the captain of our city team was exercising his dog, and he walked into the park where we were batting and bowling to each other. He came over to talk with us and asked which one was the left-hander. In cricket, often left-handers are considered prized bowlers because they sometimes have a little advantage over right-handed bowlers. He promised Daddy a start in the third-grade senior competition. Daddy was greatly tempted, but he could not accept the offer, for it would mean breaking the Sabbath, and he knew that was wrong and how much it would break our parents' hearts.

Tennis was a sport we followed least of the three. However, we both did quite well in that sport also.

It is sad for us to look back and realize we had to go to the Seventh-day Adventist school to be trapped by the idolatry of sports. It shows the great responsibility and influence of those who are in leadership positions, especially those in education who influence the next generation. This influence can be for good or for evil, for eternal life or for eternal destruction.

Ever keep in mind that one step in the wrong direction can be very difficult to overcome. It is always best not to venture onto Satan's ground, for it is much easier never to fall into sin than to gain victory over sins which have become very strong habits in the life. The Bible indicates that sports were learned by the Israelites in pagan Egypt, and the Israelites played these pagan sports when they were worshiping the golden calf.

> And they rose up early on the morrow, and offered burnt offerings, and brought peace offerings; and the people sat down to eat and to drink, and rose up to play. Exodus 32:6

Chapter 30

Later Years at School

Our class at the Newcastle Seventh-day Adventist High School was the first class to go beyond the ninth grade. It so happened that there were seven of us in that grade, and all were boys. We liked it that way, and Mr. Parr the principal liked it that way, too. It was a difficult group of young fellows, however. Even though in those days there were no street drugs, there were the temptations of alcohol and tobacco.

Beside Uncle Russell and Daddy, there was Bob Cowan. Bob's father had been brought up by a very devout Seventh-day Adventist father who had founded a termite extermination firm, which by this time, he had handed over to Bob's father, who had nothing to do with religion. However, Bob's mother was a very sweet, Christian woman. He had two sisters, one older sister, Lynette, a quite dedicated young lady, and a younger sister, Dorothy (Dot), who was quite a tomboy. Bob also was later to leave God's message.

Doug Ling, our closest friend, about a year and one-half older than Uncle Russell and Daddy, was also in that class. At this time the Ling family lived at Morpeth. To get to school he had to ride two trains which took probably close to three-quarters of an hour to get to the Hamilton Railway Station and then he had to either catch the bus from the railway station or, more likely, walk about one mile to the school. As I mentioned in an earlier story, he left the Seventh-day Adventist Church and divorced his very dedicated New Zealand wife.

Bob (Mus) Craig was in the class. Though healthy, Bob was not very strong, and he had a very weak throw when playing cricket. So

Mr. Parr sarcastically called him "Muscles," which soon became shortened to "Mus." He was about nine months older than Uncle Russell and Daddy.

Then there were two non-Seventh-day Adventists, Dennis Duggan, a rather refined young man coming from a good Protestant home. Uncle Russell and Daddy have often wondered whatever happened to him. Finally, there was Doug (Foot) Foate. His classmates called him "Foot," a derivative of Foate. For quite a number of years, though a relatively small young man, he had been a great threat to Uncle Russell and Daddy, especially being two years older. Before Uncle Russell and Daddy reached adolescence, he seemed to delight in fighting with us. If he fought with one of us, the other one would come to help, and then others would join, saying it was not fair to be two on one. Foot had the additional strength of adolescence, and we were still with the strength of preadolescent boys. We wonder what happened to him also, for neither of these two non-Seventh-day Adventists have we ever seen again since we left high school.

Like all other students within the state, when we finished the eleventh grade we were required to take the New South Wales leaving certificate state examinations in the subjects we had studied. Because our school was so small, it was not an examination center, and Uncle Russell and Daddy had to ride our bikes to Newcastle Boys' High—the premier boys' high school in Newcastle—to undertake the examinations. That in itself was somewhat of a stress simply because we were unaccustomed to being in such a large school. As it was, only four of us passed the leaving certificate examination, including Uncle Russell and Daddy. Doug Foate and Bob Cowan also passed. This immediately prepared us to attend Avondale College to begin our teacher training course.

While at the school, there were some other very sad experiences. There was a young man who came for a short time to our school. He was a troubled young man who had come from a public school. As we look back, it seems strange to us that we would take students into a Seventh-day Adventist school who had not made it in the public school, especially someone who was not a Seventh-day Adventist. Not long after, this boy committed suicide at the age of sixteen. We were absolutely stunned. That was the first time anyone we had known had committed suicide. We still remember the solemn dialogue we had with Mr. Parr over whether we had done anything to try to help the boy spiritually. Sadly, the answer was in the negative. How important it is that even very young youths seek to witness to others!

There was another troubled young man who had been expelled from the Central High School in Newcastle. He was also accepted as a student. He really amazed us. He had represented the state of New South Wales as a school boy in playing rugby, and he also was a very good cricketer. But certainly he was not ready for a Christian school. He did not last very long either.

A postscript to this story was that many years later, Grandpa and Grandma and Daddy were walking at night at the top of Newcastle, very close to Newcastle Beach, when we ran into a half drunk man who was bleeding seriously. For some reason he began to talk to Daddy of how he had a fight with his wife and how she had cut him and he needed help. The longer Daddy talked with him, the more he told about himself. Somehow, something he said indicated that he was this boy who had been at our school. Yes, he said he had attended the Newcastle Seventh-day Adventist School. What a tragedy! We would have been in our 30s when this conversation took place, and it was just a short time later that a man with his exact name (it could well have been him) was killed when a cricket ball hit him in the head as he was fielding, playing cricket. Great tragedy!

Of course, not everything was sad. Every year we had a school concert to raise money for certain projects in the school. We loved those concerts because we were able to sing and take part in all sorts of skits and plays. When Uncle Russell and Daddy look back upon it now, it was hardly the right kind of thing for a Christian School.

There was an occasion when Mr. Parr took us fishing with him by a ship wreck near Nobby's Light House, but our feeble fishing efforts were futile. None of us caught even one fish. Of course, today Uncle Russell or Daddy would not even consider fishing. It is called a sport, but it is very cruel.

We did learn some very good principles. In our tenth grade we had a very thorough course in Bible doctrines with a syllabus developed by Pastor Alfred Kranz, then the head of the Bible Department at Avondale College. The next year we had a full year course in prophecy, also following a syllabus prepared by Pastor Kranz. These were good, thorough courses which set an excellent foundation for our later learning. The Word of God is to be our daily study. It will show the way of everlasting life.

> Study to show thyself approved unto God, a workman that needeth not to be ashamed, rightly dividing the word of truth. 2 Timothy 2:15

Chapter 31

The Conversion and Baptism of Great-grandfather Bailey

Great-grandfather Bailey was born in Newcastle in 1865. However, as his name suggests, he was Irish. Indeed he was full-blooded Irish. His father, Brieley Bailey, had come with his parents from Liverpool, England to live in Australia in the 1840s, when he was seven years old. No doubt Brieley's father had worked in the industries in Liverpool. Many Irish had come to England to work during the time of the "potato famine" in the 1840s, in which the population of Ireland halved from about 8,000,000 to 4,000,000. They had come originally from Northern Ireland and were part of the Protestant Royalists.

Your Great-great-grandmother Bailey was Cathrine Brien. Her family came directly from Northern Ireland to Australia. They were also from a Protestant family. Brieley and Cathrine married in Newcastle. They had fourteen children, of which Great-grandpa Bailey was the third child. Uncle Russell and Daddy only met two of Great-grandpa Bailey's siblings—a sister, Ada, and a bachelor brother, Jim. Great-grandpa Bailey seemed to have very little to do with his family, and we recall there was quite a feud between Great-grandpa Bailey and his sister Ada, a feud that was healed after Grandpa Bailey was converted.

In the early days of living with Great-grandpa Bailey, it was very difficult for Uncle Russell and Daddy. Frequently he was complaining to Grandma about us and just as frequently Grandma was pleading with us not to upset our Grandfather. It was not that we wanted to upset him, but very quickly we would forget the warnings in our restless childhood and early youth.

We were nine years old when we moved back to the Newcastle suburb of Hamilton. Because there were only two bedrooms, Great-grandpa slept in one bedroom and Grandma and Grandpa in the other. We had to sleep in what was the dining room, straight off the kitchen.

Grandma's oldest brother, Great-uncle Oliver, lived in a tiny room off the back veranda. He never married and was not a Seventh-day Adventist. He had been a very good rugby player as a young man, but now he spent most of his time at the race course. We found out that he was an official at the race course. He also occupied his time racing pigeons, and toward the end of his life he won one of the most important pigeon races with a pigeon he had named after our sister "little Delma." I do not think he drank alcohol. Certainly if he did it was rare, but he was a chain smoker, and no doubt that hastened his death before he had reached 70 years of age. Rarely did he say much to Uncle Russell and Daddy, and it almost was as if we did not live in the same house. However, on one day he made an impact on us. We had been bantering with our father in a saucy way, and suddenly, Great-uncle Ol, as we called him, who seemed so slow and lethargic, dived at Uncle Russell and brought him to the ground with a perfect rugby tackle. We knew then that he had been a very good footballer who had been chosen to represent our city against an international touring team from England.

However, our other two surviving uncles, Great-uncle Clarence (Clarie) and Great-uncle Tom were entirely different. Great-uncle Clarie scared us very much. He always found something negative to say. We remember on one occasion we were to stay in Sydney where Great-uncle Clarie lived with his wife, Auntie Leib, who was a very delightful person. When we arrived at the house and mother knocked on the door, Great-uncle Clarie came to the door and cast his eyes on her and said, "Why didn't you come around to the back door?" We always felt uncomfortable. Once in a rare time, Great-uncle Clarie would visit back in Newcastle and come to see Great-grandpa. When Great-uncle Clarie was coming on these rare visits, Grandma pled with us to be polite and not to upset Great-uncle Clarie.

On one occasion when he came, with smiling faces Uncle Russell and Daddy greeted him with, "Good morning, Uncle." His gruff response was, "Uncle who?" Then very saintly we said, "Good morning, Uncle Clarie." That seemed to satisfy him. However, we feared him.

Great-uncle Tom was a strange bachelor. He lived in Kurri Kurri about 30 miles north of Newcastle. There for many years he delivered the mail from the Kurri Kurri post office on his bicycle. When his young brother, Great-uncle Fred, disappeared at sixteen years of age, Fred had said he was going to visit Tom. Tom claimed he never arrived. When Great-grandma Bailey went to visit Great-uncle Tom to talk about Great-uncle Fred's disappearance, Great-uncle Tom fled out the back door. There was always a great suspicion that Great-uncle Tom knew something about the disappearance of his brother. But no one will ever know if that was true until the great judgment day. When Great-grandma Bailey died, Great-grandfather contacted him and told him when the funeral would be held. Great-uncle Tom did not attend the funeral, and Great-grandpa Bailey, in great anger, disowned him as a son and would have nothing furthermore to do with him. Thus it was only many years later that we first saw our Great-uncle Tom. That was after Great-grandpa Bailey was converted and desired to make reconciliation with his son.

Grandma Bailey had been a wonderful wife for 56 years before she died. She had been a faithful Christian witness while Great-grandfather Bailey would have nothing to do with anything religious. He was a member of the Orange Lodge, which had been established after the forced abdication of King James II of Great Britain in 1688, when he converted to Catholicism and the English would not tolerate another Roman Catholic monarch. The British called William, Prince of Orange, from the Netherlands, who had married Mary, the daughter of James II, and they ruled England jointly and also vowed to protect the Protestant people of Northern Ireland. A new lodge was established called the Orangemen's Lodge. Their main loyalty was to Protestantism, and their main goal was anti-Catholicism. Uncle Russell and Daddy understand that their songs were ruthless songs against Catholics. One, we were told, talked about marching knee deep in Catholic blood. Great-grandfather Bailey had only one religion—anti-Catholicism. He hated what he called those "tykes." His hatred knew no limits. There was a Catholic family across the street from where we lived, and they had a couple of children close to our age. When we went over to play with them, Great-grandpa angrily shouted at Grandma, "Hilda, stop your kids from playing with those tykes!" We had to come home to calm Great-grandpa, and we never were able to play with them again—not because Grandma shared that hatred but because it would make Great-grandpa very angry.

Increasingly, however, we heard Great-grandpa talk about what a wonderful wife Great-grandma had been and how he loved her. She certainly had been a wonderful and faithful wife to him. Later he began to say that he wanted to see Alice (Great-grandma) again. Grandma kindly told Great-grandpa that he could only see Great-grandma again if he surrendered his life to Jesus. He knew just enough to know that God's people would go to heaven. He said he wanted to "be in heaven with Alice."

By the providence of God, the evangelist in Newcastle at that time was Pastor O.K. Anderson. Throughout his life, Great-grandpa had despised preachers, calling them parasites who lived off the money of poor people. When Pastor Anderson was a young student at Avondale College, he developed an interest in Grandma's sister who was eight years older, Great-auntie Alice. So he visited her at the family home a number of times. Somehow Great-grandpa liked him, and he did things which no one else dared to do. He called Great-grandpa "Pop." He would slap Great-grandpa on the back and ask, "Well how are you doing Pop?"

Now Pastor Anderson was an ordained minister in his 40s, and Grandma decided to ask Pastor Anderson to give Bible studies to Grandpa. No doubt Pastor Anderson was as surprised as Uncle Russell and Daddy were. He was delighted. We well remember the first day Pastor Anderson came. It was a great day. In his usual way he greeted Great-grandpa, "Well Pop, you wanted to know how you can be with Alice in heaven?" Thus began the Bible studies. It was not easy for Great-grandpa because he was now 81, and he knew so little about the Bible which Grandma had purchased for him. However, he tried to understand everything Pastor Anderson taught him. Sometimes Pastor Anderson had to teach him like a child.

One Sabbath morning, Great-grandpa appeared all dressed up in his suit, hat, walking cane, and all. So amazed was Grandma that she asked, “Where are you off to Dad?” He answered as if it was normal, “To church.” Uncle Russell and Daddy just could not imagine Great-grandpa in church. Grandma asked “How are you going to get there?” Great-grandpa responded, “Mr. Carnley is coming to take me.” He was one of a few church members who owned a car. Great-grandpa had gone to the public phone box unbeknown to the family and had asked him to take him to church. He did not miss another Sabbath including the last Sabbath before he died.

How wonderful it was when Pastor Anderson baptized him and he was voted as a member of the Hamilton Seventh-day Adventist Church! He did everything to reconcile with all he had feuded with, including his son, Great-uncle Jim. He returned his tithe regularly and gave his offerings. He also sent donations to the radio broadcast of the Voice of Prophecy. He even remembered our birthday with a present—the first time ever. At thirteen years of age we witnessed the transforming, sanctifying power of the gospel of Jesus Christ.

> For I am not ashamed of the gospel of Christ: for it is the power of God unto salvation to every one that believeth. . . . Romans 1:16

Chapter 32

What Lessons We Have Learned in Our Childhood and Early Youth

There were times when Uncle Russell and Daddy resented the strictness of their home. They felt their parents were much tougher and more controlling than the parents of their friends. In fact, there were times when we told Grandma that we wished we were children of some other parents. This was a very cruel thing to say to Grandma because she loved Uncle Russell and Daddy very much. We really loved our parents, but we felt that saying these cruel words might help us get our own way. We were self-willed boys, and we wanted our own way. However, Grandma and Grandpa never gave in to us. As we look back now on our lives, we could not have wished for better parents, and we are now thankful that they were so firm with us. Though they were very poor during our childhood and youth, nevertheless, they did everything that they thought was best not only for this life but for our eternal life.

Grandma often spoke with Uncle Russell and Daddy about how she would love for us to become pastors. We did not want to hear anything about that, for we knew we were not good enough to be pastors. We had no desire to be pastors, and we had many selfish ambitions. When Grandma would speak to us about becoming pastors, we would try to change the conversation. Never in our wildest dreams did we ever think that we would ever become pastors. Yet, Grandma lived to see Daddy ordained as a pastor, and she was so thrilled. Sadly, that was not true for

Uncle Russell, whose ordination came years after Grandma had died. However, Grandpa was alive when both of us were ordained, and in his more conservative way, we knew he was no less thankful than Grandma would have been.

Grandma was always very interested and supportive of our education. As it is with many other parents, she was always happy when we succeeded in passing our examinations. She would tell the neighbors and other relatives and even those whom she hardly knew. Even in her later life when she was working in the Sanitarium Health Food Store in Camberwell, we sometimes felt embarrassed about how she would take so much time to talk to customers about what her "boys" were doing. There was one thing certain, and that was that one of our motivations to do well was to make our parents happy. Grandpa was far more reserved than Grandma. Although he was always happy with our successes, nevertheless, as far as we know, he did not talk about his children much to others.

When Grandma died suddenly May 5, 1974, when she was only 61 years old, it was one of the saddest days of our lives. It was especially sad for Daddy because it was only one and a half days before Daddy was elected president of Columbia Union College. After her death, Daddy received his last letter from her in which she said that she was praying that the Columbia Union College board would choose a president with whom Daddy could work well. Grandma did not live to know that they chose Daddy. Neither did Grandma live to know how God led us into self-supporting work—Daddy in 1978 and Uncle Russell in 1992. Maybe on our journey to heaven we will be able to explain all this to her. However, Grandpa, who did not die until October 30, 1997, when Uncle Russell and Daddy were 64 years old, lived to know this. We were greatly encouraged by Grandpa in this work. Just a few weeks before his death, when Uncle Russell was visiting with Auntie Glenice in the United States, Grandpa in a telephone conversation solemnly asked Uncle Russell and Daddy to promise him that we would never stop preaching the precious messages which God had called us to preach. We both promised Grandpa that with God's help, we would pledge to do so. We pray that our ministries have been pleasing to God.

One of the most wonderful joys in the future, if we are faithful, will be to meet Grandma and Grandpa Standish on our way to Heaven. I am sure there will be so much to talk about. Above all, there will be the wonderful joy of all of us being together in God's kingdom. I know Uncle Russell and Daddy will be looking for their children on that same day. What a joy it will be to know that we are all together for eternity! I know God has given me the hope that our children will not be missing. Daddy pled with the Lord to give Mother and him no adoptions unless we could bring them up for the kingdom of heaven. Daddy prays daily that you will continue to dedicate your lives to Christ and His service so that we will all be together on the day of Christ's return. What a wonderful day that will be, a day that will never end!

When Grandma and Grandpa died, it was a very sad time for Uncle Russell and Daddy, but we were not in terrible despair, for we knew that if we remained faithful to Jesus, one day soon we will see them again.

> But I would not have you to be ignorant, brethren, concerning them which are asleep, that ye sorrow not, even as others which have no hope. 1 Thessalonians 4:13

Chapter 33

Going to College

When Uncle Russell and Daddy were young, like most children they did not think much about what they would do when they were grown up. By this time our father had a steady job. We knew that he was a hard worker, and, whatever he had to do, he did it conscientiously. We also greatly admired our Dad, knowing he was a very intelligent man, even though the times had not permitted him to do what he was capable of doing. He was well respected as an elder in the church and as a Sabbath school teacher and a preacher. We have always admired our father for his stability; however, it was hard to think of a profession or career when there were really no role models in our family in these areas. Indeed, we were to become the first of our known relatives since the time our first forefathers landed in Australia to finish high school. In fact, we did not even know of any family member who had completed the Intermediate certificate at the end of ninth grade. No doubt, this was because all our relatives on both sides of the family were poor.

There were other reasons, too. Grandpa had attended the little Vine Vale School across the vineyard from where he lived. It was a school which ended at seventh grade, the end of primary school in South Australia, and there was no high school anywhere near where he lived. Grandma had been forced to leave the Hamilton domestic high school part way through the eighth grade because Great-grandmother Bailey was quite ill and now was well in her 50s. Yet in spite of the frugal lifestyle which was necessary in our growing years, nevertheless Uncle

Russell and Daddy never felt deprived, for there were so many others who were in about the same situation. We do not remember when Uncle Russell and Daddy first thought much about high school and even finishing high school. However, we certainly gew into that idea. Although our parents had not had full opportunities for an education, both of them had attended Avondale College, where they met, and Grandfather attended it for more than three years and Mother for most of one year.

Grandpa and especially Grandma very strongly desired that their boys should obtain a full education. Strangely, Daddy does not remember speaking to Uncle Russell very much about what they would do in the future. Maybe it was because Grandma often told us that when we finished school we would go to Avondale College, a Seventh-day Adventist College in Australia, which was located at Cooranbong, about 30 miles from where we lived. Grandma was so determined that we would train at Avondale College that she began a bank account for us. Soon after we moved to Cardiff School when were not yet six years old, she opened this bank account for each of us, even though it was only six pence (five cents) each week from her small budget that we could bank. She had faith to believe that somehow, some way, it would help us to train for God's work when we finished high school.

So often when people would ask Uncle Russell and Daddy what we were going to do when we grew up, we would simply answer "we are going to Avondale College." Of course, they often asked what we were going to do at Avondale College, but, until a year or two before we finished high school we did not know, and we had to say that we were not sure. It truly was a strange situation for us. Sadly, we started to develop great ambitions, not toward the work for Jesus, but to become famous. When we were introduced to cricket (a game that is very popular in Australia, Britain, and the former British Colonies) we developed a great ambition to represent Australia in what is called The Test (International) matches against the English team. Both of us loved cricket, and we did well at it. However, we knew that it would be impossible to play cricket in major matches. There would always be a conflict with the Sabbath, for at that time the International matches would last for 6 days, which always included the Sabbath.

When we had reached the age of about fourteen, it was probably only our love for Grandma which kept us from seeking to fulfill our dream. How thankful we are that we had such godly Seventh-day Adventist parents who put the desire in our hearts not to displease them and make them sad!

In 1949 when there was a very exciting election for the National Parliament of Australia, we became fascinated with politics and thought it would be wonderful to become a politician or even fancied becoming Prime Minister. Yet, once again, the Sabbath was the issue. There was no way that we could be a politician, for the elections are always held on the Sabbath day in Australia. We were again thankful to Jesus that He led us away from this desire. By the time Daddy was in his later teenage years, he thought he would like to become a criminal lawyer. He eventually realized that it may not be possible to be wholly honest and truthful in this occupation. Perhaps we did not understand the full role of a lawyer, thinking mainly of being a defense lawyer, who is called a "barrister" in Australia,.

Daddy even thought about becoming a diplomat for Australia. Daddy started to fill out the application form, but once again, he realized that it would be difficult to avoid Sabbath obligations. We are thankful that God led us in His pathway.

Eventually, we did go to Avondale College. Although we did not fulfill the hopes of Grandma to train for the gospel ministry, she was pleased that we decided to enroll to be trained as Christian teachers.

We arrived at the college three weeks before school was to commence. We did not realize just how boring it is before the students return. In those three weeks, the only students who were there were those who had worked over the summer and had not gone for a break before school started. To our dismay, our first job was to pick potatoes. We first thought that we should have stayed at home where we would have continued to pick potatoes at three shillings a bag (30 cents a bag). We had been able to pick up to 20 bags in a day and commonly at least 12. At Avondale we received one shilling and four pence (13 cents) an hour. In eight hours work we received ten shillings and eight pence ($1.07). On the farms where we picked potatoes we could have earned one pound sixteen shillings ($3.60) to three pounds ($6.00) in a day.

The days seemed to pass so slowly and the evenings were so boring, but eventually the students returned and other new students arrived. Finally, we got into the routine of college life. However, being very young and immature, only a little more than 16 years old, we found the adjustment to college life difficult, and we were certainly very homesick. Now we know that that was the place which God wanted us to be to prepare us for His service, and we can say with confidence,

> And we know that all things work together for good to them that love God, to them who are called according to His purpose. Romans 8:28

Chapter 34

Shy Boys

When Uncle Russell and Daddy were very young, though we were very active and sometimes boisterous boys, we were often shy of other children and youth. We were often afraid to sit next to other children or youth about our own age because we wondered if they might not want us to sit next to them. This seems very silly now because it did not follow what the Bible says, that "A man that hath friends must shew himself friendly." (Proverbs 18:24, first part) Nevertheless we were timid to take the initiative in making friends. Perhaps we were afraid of being rejected by others, which showed our immaturity in our early teenage years. We will never forget the first time that Daddy was asked to read a short article for the Missionary Volunteer Society. Daddy was so nervous that he could hardly think, and when it was announced for him to come to present the short reading, his legs were wobbly as he went to the front. Daddy was so relieved when he had finished and had retaken his seat in the church. When we were fifteen, we were asked to help teach the juniors in the Sabbath school class. This again proved to be a very nerve racking experience for us; however, we eventually got more comfortable with that activity.

We arrived at college at sixteen years old, and we knew none of the handful of students who were there. In those days, they had tables large enough to seat eight students each, and since we were able to choose where we wanted to sit, we chose to sit together, separate from where the few other students were sitting. It was not that we did not want friends; but, at that age, we had little confidence that other students would want to be friends with us.

After several days, the matron (cafeteria director), Miss Vetter, a very kindly person, came to us and said, "You do not need to sit by yourselves. Come with me and I will introduce you to some of the other students." We did not want to do that, but we had no other alternative but to let her introduce us to some of the students. Thereafter, fearing that Miss. Vetter would see us eating alone, we did go to sit by other students, and soon we began to get to know them a little. It seemed that college was full of many challenges, and we wondered whether we would get used to our new situation. It was a growing experience for teenagers to learn to put away self-defense and learn to reach out in friendship to others. The Bible says:

> A man that hath friends must show himself friendly: and there is a friend [Jesus] that sticketh closer than a brother. Proverbs 18:24 (Brackets supplied)

Chapter 35

New Experiences

When Uncle Russell and Daddy got involved in their teaching course at Avondale College, they did not really understand the name of the course. It was called The Theological Normal Course. It was called a "normal" course because that was the name commonly given to teacher training during the nineteenth century and until the middle of the twentieth century. It was also called The Theological Educational Course. This name was to make it easier for teachers graduating from Avondale College to be classified as exempt from service in the military. This title was added during the Second World War. The Roman Catholic Church had asked for exemption from military service for their teaching brothers, such as the Marist and Christian brothers. However, the government could not give exemption to the Roman Catholic teaching brothers unless they also gave exemption for other Christian teachers in Protestant schools.

Soon after Daddy and Uncle Russell commenced their teacher training, the Australian government decided to draft all young men into military training once they reached the age of eighteen. When the Korean War broke out in 1951, many of these drafted young men were sent to fight in the Australian army in Korea. We turned eighteen about three weeks before we graduated. This meant that we would normally have been called up in the Australian army and possibly sent to serve in Korea. Of course, we did not believe in fighting, but we would have followed the recommendation of the leaders of the Seventh-day Adventist Church in Australia and asked to train in a medical unit. However, because Uncle Russell and Daddy were committed to teach in Seventh-day Adventist schools in New South Wales, we were exempt from the military draft. Thus we could accept our appointments. Uncle Russell went to teach at Mumble Peg in western New South Wales, and Daddy at Ophir Glen, on the far north coast of New South Wales.

Very soon after our first college year had started, we were taken to the Avondale Primary School (an elementary school) to observe different teachers teaching their classes. The school had four teachers. Miss Doble, who was the youngest teacher in the school, though still quite experienced, taught the first and second grades; Miss Schnaple taught grades three and four; and the Principal, Mr. Shepard, taught the fifth and sixth grades. Miss Nieber taught what was called the rural school class, which was set up like a small, one teacher school with students in all grades from first grade to sixth grade. However, it was not until our second year of training that we observed and taught in the rural classroom. We had to first learn how to teach in the rooms which had only one or two grades.

After observing a few classes by the teachers, we were then listed to teach our first practice lesson. Daddy cannot forget the first class which he taught. Maybe all new teacher trainees are a little nervous for their first day teaching; however, I think Uncle Russell and Daddy may have been the most nervous. Daddy was given the task of teaching the letter "q" to the first grade students. We had to write out a lesson plan and have it approved by the director, Doctor Geoffrey Rosenhain.

Daddy remembers how nervous he was just waiting outside the door for the first class which he was to teach. Eventually, Miss Doble invited me in, introduced Daddy to the class, and told the students that she wanted them to listen carefully to what Daddy had to say. The class was to be for a half hour, and Daddy had spent many hours preparing for it. After ten minutes Daddy thought that he had almost finished what he had prepared; however, somehow he was able to see out the whole 30 minutes. What a great relief it was when the time was up! When Miss Doble came out to give Daddy a little evaluation of his efforts, she burst into laughter. She realized just how timid and nervous Daddy had been.

With the Lord's help, the next week Daddy had to teach a history lesson to the fifth and sixth grades of Mr. Shepard. Daddy was even more nervous, for these were older children, and before he was invited in to teach the class he could hear Mr. Shepard telling the students very strongly that he wanted them to obey and listen as Daddy taught. After that lesson, Daddy thought he had done a little better. Of course, it eventually became routine, as every week we had a class for which to prepare.

New changes came in the second year. We now had to train with Miss Nieber in the multi-grade classroom. Miss Nieber, had all the characteristics of her German background. She had been born in Tonga, an island kingdom in the South Pacific, which was a German colony at the time Miss Neiber was born. She was very kind and helpful to Uncle Russell and Daddy, and we learned to respect her very highly. She was a wonderful teacher and also firm with the children, but they loved her, and it was amazing how many parents wanted their children to go into the rural classroom so that they would have the experience of Miss Nieber. Both Uncle Russell and Daddy learned a great deal from Miss Nieber. Later we became good friends with her when she was well in her 80s and then into her 90s. Miss Nieber was a woman of great love for God and for His truth, and she had a very dignified bearing. She often attended our meetings when we spoke in or near Cooranbong.

In the second year, every student in the class had to present a "discussion" lesson in which the chairman of the education department, Doctor Rosenhain, along with all the students in the same college class would listen to the lesson. After the lesson, each one was able to make comments about the lesson—what they saw that was good and what they felt could have been done to improve the presentation. Somehow this peer evaluation seemed even more challenging than the evaluation of the lesson by the class teacher or even the department chairman.

While we were in our second year, we were sent away from college for practice teaching in other Seventh-day Adventist schools. Though this was an entirely different environment with different supervision, it helped us to teach in an effective way.

There were other experiences which were difficult for Uncle Russell and Daddy. On a couple of occasions we were asked to give the worship at the young men's dormitory. We worked so hard to prepare for those worships. In these talks, Daddy was very nervous. At one worship he was talking about the power of the sacrifice of Christ and he started it by saying "This is well said in the hymn . . ." and suddenly Daddy's mind went blank. He does not know how many seconds went by before it suddenly came back to him and he was able to finish the quote by saying "There's Power in the Blood." Daddy is sure you remember that hymn. Even more challenging was the invitation to give a talk at the young ladies' evening worship, but God was good, and Daddy made it through.

In our second year we took the class in homiletics, which is a course to help you to learn how to preach. Pastor Nelson Burns was our teacher—a very fine man. In those days, every student in the homiletics class had to make a presentation at chapel. However, it was not on his own. Pastor Burns divided us into groups of three. We would then have to decide who would give the first part, who would give the middle part, and who would give the last part of the sermon. Pastor Burns assigned Uncle Russell, Daddy, and their best friend, Milton Sibley, to be one team. I well remember the text which he gave to us, for we had no choice. The text was Romans 2:14, 15:

> For when the Gentiles, which have not the law, do by nature the things contained in the law, these, having not the law, are a law unto themselves: which show the work of the law written in their hearts, their conscience also bearing witness, and their thoughts the mean while accusing or else excusing one another.

Daddy gave the first part, Milton the second, and Uncle Russell the third. It was so nerve racking because this was a presentation made before all the faculty and all the student body at the college. However, we remember how Pastor Burns encouraged us. We had walked partway up the steps of the chapel, waiting for the appropriate time to walk in and to the front, and as we were standing there, Pastor Burns turned to the three of us and said, "O how I wish your parents were here to hear you today!" Somehow it gave us confidence that Pastor Burns felt we would do well. The theme which we presented was centered around the conscience and the importance of our consciences to help us make right or wrong decisions. What a blessing these experiences were as we began to gain confidence in presenting God's Word! The Bible talks about teachers and preachers very frequently. There is one text which emphasizes both preaching and teaching:

> Preaching the kingdom of God, and teaching those things which concern the Lord Jesus Christ, with all confidence, no man forbidding him. Acts 28:31

Chapter 36

Evangelistic Crusades

When Uncle Russell and Daddy were boys and youth, we attended many evangelistic crusades. In those days in Australia, pastors were not assigned to churches; their primary role was to bring souls to the Lord. Thus every year either in the city or in different suburbs of Newcastle, evangelists would hold six-month-long crusades which would begin either in February or March and go through the Australian autumn and winter. Often in those days, the crusades were conducted only on Sunday nights or at most, twice a week. Each other night of the week the evangelist conducted Bible studies in the homes of interested people.

When we were nine years old, we began attending the Hamilton church in Newcastle, and very soon after that we were involved in the crusades. The evangelist would come to our church, preach a sermon, and tell us of his plans for the crusade and how he needed the help of all the church members. The evangelist would have printed many thousands of advertisements announcing his crusade. On Sabbath afternoons, all those who were willing to help would fold the announcements so that they could be ready to place in letterboxes.

The next Sabbath afternoon, we distributed the leaflet, and we were eager to help even when we were young. Sometimes two or more different announcements were sent out, and sometimes another announcement was sent out after the crusade had commenced.

We remember when we were about thirteen years of age, Pastor O.K. Anderson was conducting a series of meetings. With Grandpa and

Grandma we went to the hall, helped to sweep and clean it, and then set out chairs for the meeting. However, these crusades were usually held in tents. Now, because much of the crusade was over the winter time, those tents had to be heated. The tent floor would be covered with straw or sawdust and, when needed, the tent was heated by kerosene heaters. Today that would not be permitted because of the risk of fire. However, we do not remember any problems whatsoever. Although perhaps it was not very healthy, you can understand why the people tried to huddle as close as they could to the kerosene heaters, despite the strong kerosene odor, for that was better than shivering in the tent.

Uncle Russell and Daddy loved crusades, and Grandpa and Grandma were also usually very actively involved . In some crusades, Grandma was the pianist. Grandpa was usually an usher and a greeter and got to know the people attending fairly well. Of course, we loved to go along with them. We especially loved to hear about the prophecies—the big image of Daniel 2, the beasts of Daniel 7 and 8, and so on. We would learn about the Sabbath and of Jesus' ministry as our High Priest in the heavenly sanctuary. We learned about the three angels' messages, what the Bible said about death being like a sleep, and many other interesting things which are found in the Bible.

We were always very interested to see how many people who were not Seventh-day Adventists attended each meeting. We would be sad when the numbers lessened as the crusade continued. Of course, we were very happy when some of the interested people would begin to attend our church and then later when they were baptized. We listened to many evangelists—whose names you do not know but which we will always remember: Pastor Eddie Rosendahl, Pastor John Conley, Pastor Edwin Jewson, Pastor Donald Whittaker, Pastor Brian Reynolds, and Pastor O.K. Anderson, and others.

The evangelist we remember best, however, was Pastor George Burnside. We do not remember any evangelistic crusade held by pastors before Pastor Burnside conducted his crusade in Newcastle in 1951. Newcastle was a very difficult city. It was the industrial capital of Australia, so people were mainly working class people, and many of them were not very interested in religion. Some even called Newcastle "the graveyard of evangelists," meaning that it was very difficult to bring people to the Lord. At every evangelistic crusade, however, there were a few people who would accept the precious truths which God has given to the Seventh-day Adventist Church.

Pastor Burnside, I remember, was then 43 years of age. He had had conducted wonderfully successful crusades in many of the big cities in New Zealand and Australia. However, the Seventh-day Adventists in Newcastle were shocked when Pastor Burnside was assigned to conduct a crusade in Newcastle, where so few were likely to be baptized. Because so many church members had little faith, they felt Pastor Burnside would not succeed any more than the other evangelists before him, because all of them were good evangelists. Some even said that Pastor Burnside would "meet his Waterloo in Newcastle." Now American young people reading this book may not understand what that statement means, but it was at the Battle of Waterloo in 1815 that Napoleon was finally defeated and was captured and sent to live in exile on the little island of St. Helena, off the west coast of Africa. So they were meaning that Pastor Burnside, as an evangelist, would meet with defeat in Newcastle.

This rumor reached the ears of Pastor Burnside himself. When Pastor Burnside preached for the first time in the Hamilton church, before the start of the crusade, he paused for a little while and scanned all the people in that church. The church was absolutely packed, for other members came from the smaller churches around. Everyone, including Uncle Russell and Daddy, wondered why he was hesitating to speak after he walked to the pulpit, but then he said in a very challenging voice, "I hear that some of you are saying that Burnside will meet his Waterloo in Newcastle. Well, I want to tell you something. Burnside might well meet his Waterloo in Newcastle, but I don't believe God will meet His Waterloo. My text today is . . ." The people were shocked, yet strangely inspired.

Many felt very embarrassed because they had not wanted Pastor Burnside to know what they had said, for Pastor Burnside was a great man of faith. At the time Pastor Burnside presented this crusade, we were second year students at Avondale College, and therefore we only attended a few of the meetings, yet we were greatly electrified by what he preached. What a wonderful preacher! He knew God's message, and he knew God. He preached the message with power and certainty as Jesus did. He knew his Bible so well that the people of Newcastle were greatly impressed by the messages which he presented. They thought he knew where every text of the Bible was found.

In the end, Pastor Burnside baptized more than 130 people, a number that has never been approached in Newcastle before or after Pastor Burnside's crusade. He was a great man of faith, and God richly blessed his ministry. Daddy desires that you grow up to be a man and a woman of faith, and he desires that you grow up to accept the charge that Paul gave to young Timothy:

> I charge thee therefore before God, and the Lord Jesus Christ, who shall judge the quick and the dead at His appearing and His kingdom; preach the word; be instant in season, out of season; reprove, rebuke, exhort with all longsuffering and doctrine. For the time will come when they will not endure sound doctrine; but after their own lusts shall they heap to themselves teachers, having itching ears; and they shall turn away their ears from the truth, and shall be turned unto fables. But watch thou in all things, endure afflictions, do the work of an evangelist, make full proof of thy ministry. 2 Timothy 4:1–5

Chapter 37

Baptism

When Uncle Russell and Daddy were boys, we witnessed a number of baptisms in the Hamilton church in Newcastle, where we worshipped from the age of nine to sixteen.

Under the Sabbath school platform, which was below and in front of the platform used for church service, there was a small baptismal font. In those days, baptism services were far more significant than today, where, at least in the United States, they usually hold a baptism just before the beginning of the divine service. When we were boys, it was a full meeting, and it was always held on Sabbath afternoon in place of the young people's meetings.

Whenever there was a baptism we looked forward to it. Usually it was just one or two people to be baptized, but in those days baptisms were always very significant. The Pastor would preach a full sermon on a topic which explained some aspect of baptism, what it meant and its importance. Sometimes the baptism was of someone who had grown up in the church, but on other occasions it was of someone who had been led to the church in an evangelistic crusade or by a church member. If a church member had studied with the one to be baptized, he or she was especially excited. The one who had led them to God's message usually had some part to play in the baptism, even if it was simply explaining how the studies had begun and how the person had responded.

It became even more exciting for us if it was a baptism of someone whom Grandpa had led to the Lord. Grandpa always sought to have at least one person with whom he was studying the Bible. Of course, sadly, not all accepted the wonderful message of salvation and the Seventh-day Adventist faith. Yet, when someone did accept God's end-time message and was baptized, we were very excited about it.

However, the most surprising baptism we remember was not that of one whom Grandpa brought to the Lord. It involved a baptism where three or four young people were to be baptized. The evangelist in Newcastle at that time was Pastor O.K. Anderson. (You will remember meeting him when we visited Australia. Pastor O.K. Anderson passed away at 95 years of age in 2001. You will remember visiting him in the hospital a few months before he died.)

Among those to be baptized was a young woman who had reached the age of twenty. However, the church members and especially the leaders of the church had been very concerned about her because she was keeping company with a sailor named Alfie who was not a Seventh-day Adventist and was not even a practicing Christian. Alfie's family name was Seaman (a very appropriate name for a sailor). When she joined the baptismal class and told Alfie, he became very upset and tried to urge her not to be baptized. Later, when she told him she was to be baptized, he became very angry and threatened to harm her if she did not change her decision. Yet, in spite of the fact that some of the church members had believed that she was not a very strong Christian, she was determined to be baptized, and she refused to change her mind because of Alfie's threats. The church members felt very concerned for her but were very grateful that she was standing so firm.

Then, the Sabbath afternoon came for the baptism. The ladies changed in the back room on the right-hand side facing the pulpit, and the young men changed on the left-hand side of the pulpit. As we continued to sing hymns, the young ladies seated themselves in their place on the front row of the church, but the young men had not come to take their place, and neither had Pastor Anderson. We wondered what was the holdup, but eventually the door opened, and Pastor Anderson came out with not one, but two men. The church had only understood one young man was to be baptized. The shock was greatest when we realized that the second young man was Alfie. He was easy to pick out because he was a very short man, and quite a number of us had seen him before. No one could understand why he was sitting among the baptismal group. However, nothing was said, and Pastor Anderson led out in the service before the baptism.

We were sure that almost everyone in the church was wondering why Alfie was there sitting with the other young man to be baptized. We know the elders were quite surprised, for Grandpa was an elder. They and the church board had knowledge of the other candidates which they had approved, but they had no idea of Alfie. All they knew was that Alfie had threatened his girlfriend if she went ahead with her baptism.

After his sermon, Pastor Anderson went down into the pool, and he called for the first young lady to come to be baptized. After she was baptized, he called for the first young man to come into the pool to be baptized. Then he called for Alfie and his girlfriend to come into the pool together. The church members were shocked. However, before he conducted the baptism, Pastor Anderson explained what had happened. While he and the other young man were changing to prepare for the baptism, suddenly Alfie came to the side door of the back room and said, "I want to be baptized, too."

Pastor Anderson attempted to explain to him that he would be very happy to give him Bible studies and prepare him for baptism in the future, but Alfie said, "No, I want to be baptized today with my girlfriend." Pastor Anderson reminded Alfie of the threat which he had made to his girlfriend. Alfie responded with great repentance, admitting that he had angrily threatened his girlfriend. He had truly expected her to withdraw from the baptism, but when he realized that she was determined to go ahead with the baptism in spite of his threats, it was more than he could imagine, and it made him realize just how important baptism was to his girlfriend. The Holy Spirit clearly spoke to Alfie. His heart was softened, and now he wanted to be baptized.

Pastor Anderson did not know what to do. He had never faced a situation like this before, and he never did afterwards. He asked, "Alfie, what do you know about the Seventh-day Adventist faith?" Alfie told him that Seventh-day Adventists did not eat pork, and that they worshipped on Saturday. This hardly seemed an adequate body of understanding of God's precious truths for baptism; nevertheless, here he was in the baptismal pool. Uncle Russell and Daddy remember very well how people would say they thought Pastor Anderson did the wrong thing, and as boys we thought he had done the wrong thing, too. However, that day Alfie was baptized with the young woman who was to become his wife.

The pastor agreed that it was an extraordinarily unusual situation, but by the grace of God Alfie became a very fine Seventh-day Adventist. He became a great missionary worker and led others to the Lord. The last time Daddy met him, many years ago, he was an elder of the Lithgow church and doing a wonderful work for God. The Holy Spirit prompted Pastor Anderson to baptize him in spite of his limited knowledge of the Seventh-day Adventist faith. Of course, this would not be a normal example for preparation, for Sister White tells us that we need to be thoroughly prepared for baptism. However, this baptism greatly moved Uncle Russell and Daddy.

It was not too long after this that Pastor R.A.R. Thrift was the pastor in the Newcastle region. We were now fifteen years of age, and Pastor Thrift had been a vice-president of what we now call the South Pacific Division. With a small baptismal class of about half a dozen, which included Uncle Russell and Daddy, we went through many weeks of study. Pastor Thrift was very thorough in his preparation of this group of young people. We knew the beliefs of the church quite well, much better than the other candidates because we came from a very strong home. We had been attending church all our lives, and at school we had learned much of the Bible.

Eventually the time came when Pastor Thrift set a date for the baptism, and he fully expected that Uncle Russell and Daddy would be baptized, but though we knew so much, we realized that we had not surrendered our hearts to Jesus, and therefore we surprised him by saying that we were not planning to be baptized. He was very concerned because, being then in his 60s and like a grandfather to us, he was earnestly concerned about our soul salvation. He visited us in our home at 78 Dumaresq Street, but we continued to tell him that we were not ready for baptism. So, with sadness, he left the house, but the baptism did go forward with the other candidates.

At the end of that year we had turned sixteen years of age, and we had completed high school. Early the next year, 1950, we attended Avondale College. It was toward the end of the year that we learned that Pastor Thrift was conducting another baptism in the Hamilton church. Uncle Russell and Daddy talked it over, and we decided there and then that we would go forward in baptism, and we decided that Pastor Thrift was the man we wanted to baptize us. This time it was different. We had not even told our parents, so when we arrived home on Friday afternoon, they were certainly surprised to see us and wondered why we had come home for the weekend. Remember, we only lived about 30 miles away from Avondale College; however, the rules were strict and we did not get home very often.

Because we had no telephone, there was no way to tell Pastor Thrift before Sabbath morning that we were planning to be baptized. When we went to talk to him about it, he was so thrilled! We could tell how much he earnestly wanted us to be ready for God's Kingdom. It was a surprise to the other church members, although not nearly as much a surprise as the baptism of Alfie. On that Sabbath afternoon in October, just a week or two before we turned seventeen, we were baptized into the family of God and into the Seventh-day Adventist truth and church. How thankful we are that God was so patient with us and did not give up on us! It was a great blessing for us to go forward in baptism, and we have never regretted doing so, for the Bible tells us,

> Repent, and be baptized every one of you in the name of Jesus Christ for the remission of sins, and ye shall receive the gift of the Holy Ghost. Acts 2:38

Chapter 38

Homesickness and Financial Woes

Very soon after Uncle Russell and Daddy had gone to Avondale College we were very homesick. We were only sixteen years of age. Though there were times when we thought we were unhappy at home, when we left for college we realized just how much home meant to us and how good our parents had been to us.

After all the ten years of saving that our mother had put aside for us to go to college, we still had only about 50 pounds ($100) each. Even in 1950, that was a small amount of money for fees in a boarding college, and we were shocked when we received an account statement six weeks after school had begun and realized that all that money had been used up. We could not imagine how big our debt would be by the end of the year. Later we realized that, at that time, our small earnings at college had not yet been applied to our college account, but it was still a daunting situation.

Our parents were in no way able to help us. By this time Auntie Delma had been born, and of course, they had to care for her. We also believed that we would not be able to raise all the money that would be needed to pay off the debt. That together with the homesickness which we experienced led us to decide the best thing was to leave college, go back home, work somewhere for the rest of the year, and then next year go to the New South Wales State Teachers' College to train.

We had both received scholarships when we finished high school to attend the teachers' college. This would pay for all our fees, including textbooks and other supplies. It would have paid for our accommodation in the teachers' college, and it would also have given us an allowance for food. We thought this would be the wise thing to do. Thus, we decided to make a phone call.

We telephoned the Sanitarium Health Food Company where Grandpa worked and left a message requesting him to ask Grandma to call us back at college the next day at a set time. We waited for the call, and, sure enough, your dutiful Grandma called us. She could not understand why we would telephone her. We had no telephone at home so she had to ride her bicycle to the Sanitarium Health Food Company to make the call. She felt there must be something up for us to take this unusual action. So with some degree of anxiety in her voice, she asked what the problem was.

We explained to her the predicament we were in regarding our financial situation. She listened, and we told her of our plan to leave, come home, and then the following year go to the state teachers' college. There was a moment of silence. Then Grandma uttered these words: "Boys, we haven't sacrificed all these years for you to go to a secular school. You stay there. That is where I want you to be." We tried to answer her by saying, "How can we ever pay off this money? The only thing to do would be to take off next year and work to pay it back. Maybe even then we would not have enough money to go back the next year." Yet when Grandma spoke we knew there would be no changing her decision, and so we stayed at Avondale College.

Of course, at the end of the year, we had a very large debt. We returned home quickly when college ended for the year. Immediately Grandma said, "Well boys, you have to get a job." Of course, we already understood that would be the case. "But where can we get a job?" was our question. Grandma responded, "Some Adventist boys have worked at Newbold Brick Factory, and they seem to have earned some good money. Get on your bicycles and ride over and find the personnel officer and see if he will give you a job."

Newbold Brick Factory was the biggest industrial brick factory in the Southern Hemisphere. It employed well over six hundred workers, and it was located about four miles from our home. It made many tens of millions of bricks every year to line the tunnels through which molten steel would pass in the huge steel mills which were located not far from the brick factory.

We arrived at the factory and located the personnel office. Timidly, we knocked on the door, and a strong voice said, "Come in." We felt very intimidated as Mr. Scott, a rather large man in his late thirties, greeted us. He proved to be a friendly man who put us at ease as we tried to explain to him that we desired to have a job so that we could earn fees to go back to the Christian college where we were training to be teachers. We believe that the Holy Spirit went before us, and God was rewarding the faith of Grandma. Mr. Scott responded by saying, "You fellows look strong. I tell you what I will do for you. If you can work like men, I will pay you a man's salary."

We could not believe our ears. We had just recently turned seventeen years of age. At that time seventeen year olds would not earn much more than a third the salary of a twenty-one year old. When he told us what the salary was, it was considerably more than our father was earning. He then told us that the men worked hard to obtain group bonuses for Christmas and that we would be expected to work hard to help earn these bonuses. We assured him that we would do our best.

It was certainly hard work wheeling wet bricks into the kiln to be baked. We used very specialized barrows—a square front and a flat base without sides. We were expected to put about five hundred pounds of brick on every barrow load, but because of the way the barrows were balanced, it did not feel excessively heavy. However, we had to wheel them along narrow metal tracks to the kiln. If we deviated in any way from the metal tracks, the barrow would automatically begin to tip over. At first, we tipped quite a few barrows, but again, with the help of the Lord, we were soon able to be effective wheelers and were able to produce as did the older workers.

Beside Uncle Russell and Daddy, another man started the same day, but he did not last long. We knew we had to last, because we had to pay back our debts to the College and try to earn money to go to school the next year, and this we did.

The men worked to earn a 50% bonus above their salary before Christmas, and after Christmas they dropped it back to working for a

30% bonus. Even when earning a 50% bonus, the men only worked to 2:30 pm. They spent the rest of the time until the 4:00 pm knock-off time playing cards. An "understanding" foreman did not come by after the afternoon tea break. Of course, they worked hard for the first six and a half hours of "work" time. Not only were we able to pay back all our debt, but we were able to deposit over 100 pounds (more than $200) to start the new school year, more than twice what we had the previous year.

We faced a situation at the brick factory we had never faced before. The conversation of the other workers was so vile. They swore, cursed, used dirty language and worst of all, took God's name in vain. Another Seventh-day Adventist boy two years older than us got together with us before work began every day and prayed that God would keep our language pure. God was good, and none of us failed. These men would make fun of us, but we did not fail in our loyalty to God. Several years later, a non-Seventh-day Adventist cousin by marriage worked with these men, and we were quite surprised to hear that they told him how they admired us.

Of course, we did not use the money we earned for anything else. We would take our pay packets home to Grandma, and after taking tithe and offering out, the rest would be deposited into a bank account. We were certainly taught to be responsible and frugal with money.

At the end of our second and graduating year, we both had a debt, but it was only 25-26 pounds ($50-52). The business manager asked us what our plans were to pay it off. We told him we would pay it back before Christmas. He was quite surprised, as graduation took place just after the middle of November. He told us he would give us to the end of January. We told him he would have the money before Christmas, and that he did. Of course, we went back to Newbold brick factory, and again Mr. Scott readily reemployed us. He told us that he had heard that we had done well the year before.

It is very important for you to learn the lesson that when you have a responsibility, do it well by doing the very best you can. What a wonderful blessing it was, and what a lesson it was to Uncle Russell and Daddy to see how God provides when we do the best we can!

I often wonder what we would have done in life had we gone to the state teachers' training college and taught in public schools. God called us to be His servants to train others and bring others to the knowledge of God and to the kingdom of heaven. Remember that God has claims upon your service which are paramount.

> But my God shall supply all your need according to his riches in glory by Christ Jesus. Philippians 4:19

CHAPTER 39

Graduation

After the first several months at Avondale College, we began to get used to being away from home, and we were able to make friends with other students. We had to work hard for 20 hours a week to help cover our fees. As we have told you, God worked wonderfully for us as He will for anyone who follows His guidance and leading.

The second year, unfortunately, we did not always follow the principles that had been laid down at Avondale College, and therefore there were times when we had to face the discipline committee. By God's mercy and grace, we were never penalized for what we had done. We believed that God had His care over us as passionate youth. We had no real idea of what God had planned for our lives, and I know that you have no idea of what God has planned for your lives, but He has a special plan for you as He did for Uncle Russell and Daddy.

The second year we worked in the Sanitarium Health Food Company which is located close to the college. It was not easy work for both of us, as our work involved standing for four hours every day that we worked. Yet, hard work is not something to be avoided. As we came to the end of the school year, we started to wonder whether or not we would receive an appointment to teach in one of the Seventh-day Adventist schools. Like all other young people who hoped to be employed in denominational service, we were interviewed by the denominational educational director of the Trans-Tasman Conference, Pastor Benjamin McMahon, and by Pastor Harold Heath, the educational director of the

Trans-Commonwealth Union. They gave us no indication of whether or not they would place us in any of our schools.

Eventually, shortly before graduation, the lists went up. To our great relief and joy both of us received an appointment. All we knew, however, was that Uncle Russell had been appointed to the Trans-Commonwealth Union, and Daddy had been appointed to the Trans-Tasman Union. This meant we could be sent a long way from each other. The Trans-Commonwealth Union included the South New South Wales, Victorian, Tasmanian, South Australian, and West Australian Conferences. The Trans-Tasman Conference included the North Queensland (now North Australian), Queensland (now South Queensland), Northern New South Wales, Greater Sydney, North New Zealand, and the South New Zealand Conferences. We still had great uncertainty of where we would be placed in those regions.

Eventually Uncle Russell received the information that he was to serve in the South New South Wales Conference, and Daddy received word that he was to serve in the North New South Wales Conference, so we were not going to be as far away from each other as we thought we might be. But, we still did not know the schools until eventually sometime after graduation we were told the school to which we were appointed.

Both of us were appointed to one-teacher schools. Uncle Russell was appointed to the Mumble Peg School, a little school with eight students in Western New South Wales where the farmers raised wheat and sheep and grew oranges. It was not far away from the town of Narromine. Daddy was assigned to the Ophir Glen School, near Burringbar, not far from the Queensland boarder in the north coast region of New South Wales. He found that he had fourteen students. All the parents were banana growers, but Daddy is getting a little ahead of the story.

After the excitement of discovering where we were going to teach, we concentrated on preparation for graduation. We knew that this would be a very solemn occasion, and we looked forward to it with great anticipation, especially since we knew how overjoyed Grandpa and Grandma would be to see us graduate. Indeed, it proved to be a very proud and happy moment for them. Of course, no doubt other parents of graduates were just as proud, happy and thankful to God.

Graduating at the same time were young ladies who were also identical twins. They were the daughters of Pastor and Mrs. Herbert White. Pastor White was later to serve in the General Conference in the Lay Activities Department (now called Personal Ministries) before retiring. Because of the uniqueness of having two sets of identical twins graduating, the organizers of the graduation chose the White twins to march with Uncle Russell and Daddy. Uncle Russell partnered Evonne, and Daddy partnered Veronica.

We had never attended a graduation before, for we had no graduations when we finished primary school or secondary school. The graduation was held in a large tent on campus in front of the chapel. One of the main speakers for our graduation was Dr. Weniger. He was then a professor at Pacific Union College in the United States and was known as one of the most effective speakers in God's church at that time. Indeed, he taught speech to the students. The other speaker was Pastor Eric Hare, the famed missionary to Burma (now called Myanmar). Perhaps there has never been as great a story teller as Pastor Hare. I well remember that the last time I saw him was in the Sligo Church downstairs, telling one of his fascinating Burma stories to the children of that generation. This was in the late 1970s and not long before his death. Of course, we were fascinated by his presentations also.

Thus began our ministry for God. How Daddy prays that your ministry for God will be as rewarding and as blessed as have been Uncle Russell's and Daddy's ministries! No, Daddy prays that you will accomplish far greater things for God than ever Uncle Russell or Daddy have. All we can say is that God has been so good to us. He has guided us all through these years, and we can only praise His name. May that also be your experience.

> Go ye therefore, and teach all nations, baptizing them in the name of the Father, and of the Son, and of the Holy Ghost: teaching them to observe all things whatsoever I have commanded you: and, lo, I am with you alway, even unto the end of the world. Amen. Matthew 28:19, 20

Index

Scripture References

Spirit of Prophecy References

Institutions

People

Topics

Hartland Publications Book List

These books may be ordered from Hartland Publications (see the last page of this book for complete contact information). Many of these books are also available from Highwood Books in Australia: 03–59637011

Books by Colin Standish and Russell Standish

(Unless otherwise noted as by one or the other)

The 144,000, the Great Multitude, and the Return of Jesus

Fascinating as it has been to many Christians, few have solved the mystery of the 144,000 and the great multitude of the book of Revelation. Yet the pioneers of the Seventh-day Adventist Church focused much attention upon them. Like a sudden and unexpected flash of blinding lightning the 144,000 are introduced in Revelation 7 and again in Revelation 14, never again to be mentioned. The Old Testament is silent on the topic; Christ said nothing about it; neither did the writers of the gospels or the apostolic epistles. Yet the authors solve most of the divisive interpretations from the Bible itself and show how important is the understanding of these groups to all Christians.

Adventism Imperiled—Education in Crisis (230 pages)

In this newly revised edition of the most penetrating books written on Adventist education, the Standish brothers go directly to the word of God for the principles by which children that are called to be the sons and daughters of the King of the universe are to be educated. Every

Seventh-day Adventist interested in our children and youth should read this book. Both authors are trained educators, having spent decades in education from the elementary to university level.

Adventism Proclaimed (202 pages)

In answer to "When shall these things be and what shall be the sign of thy coming, and the end of the world?" (Matthew 24:3), Jesus related many signs. One of those signs (verse 14) has captivated the authors—"This gospel of the kingdom shall be preached in all the world for a witness unto all nations: and then shall the end come." In the context of the 3 Angels Messages, this is what shall go forth with the power of the loud cry of Revelation 18:1–5. "To every nation, and kindred, and tongue and people." (Revelation 14:6) You will feel compelled to share with others, and be motivated to prepare urgently for the coming of the Lord.

Adventism Vindicated (141 pages)

The late 1970s was a time when the new theology was rapidly engulfing a confused and uncertain Seventh-day Adventist Church as a reaction to legalistic principles. Tragically, many who found the impotency of legalism were deceived into accepting a theology that claims that there are no divine conditions of salvation–a belief that victorious Christian living is not possible and has no mandate in salvation. This book answers the writings of Jack Sequeira as they relate to the precious message of "Christ our Righteousness" given at the 1888 General Conference in Minneapolis.

The Antichrist Is Here (185 pages)

A newly updated, second edition! Colin and Russell Standish have extensively researched the historical identification of the antichrist of past generations and are convinced the antichrist is present on earth now. They have taken those events which have transpired in the last decade and measured them in the light of biblical prophecy. You will read undeniable evidence in support of their findings. A "must-read" for those who are interested in biblical prophecy and its outworking in contemporary history.

The Big Bang Exploded (218 pages)

For decades the "big bang" hypothesis has held sway as the dominant explanation of the origin of the universe. It has proven to be a remarkably enduring hypothesis, yet the determined efforts of scientists from many disciplines have failed to provide confirmation of this hypothesis.

The authors assert that the "big bang theory" and Darwin's proposal of natural selection are "spent, decayed and archaic theories." The Standish brothers seriously address some of the most startling challenges to this theory of origins. They present evidence which they assert supports, far more closely, the fiat creation concept than the evolutionary model. This is another of the increasing challenges which evolutionary scientists must address if their credibility is not to be seriously undermined.

Deceptions of the New Theology (290 pages)

The term "new theology" was made prominent in the 1970s with the presentation by a number of popular preachers in the Seventh-day Adventist Church who taught what appeared to many to be a beautiful, new, Christ-centered emphasis. However, the ultimate results have been seen in untold thousands leaving the Seventh-day Adventist church, including many ministers and denominational workers. The answer to the eternal destructiveness of this movement is to uphold the authentic Christ.

Education for Excellence (174 pages)

This book goes directly to the word of God for educational principles for the sons and daughters of the King of the Universe. In the ministry of the apostle Paul, the culture, philosophy and education of paganism was confronted by the principles of God-given education. Though the world of his day was under the political rulership of Rome, Greece still controlled the mind, and therefore the educational processes of the Mediterranean. As Paul's ministry led him to city after city under the influence of Greek education and philosophy, it was necessary for him to define clearly the differences between pagan and Christian education. Most cultures today face the continued influence of paganistic education. Many who claim to support Christian education nevertheless are not fully aware of the complete contrasts between the two. Christianity wholly defines the curriculum, the teacher selection, the teaching methodology, the extracurricular activities, etc. Its goals, purposes and objectives are entirely different from secular education.

Embattled Church (143 pages)

The SDA church faces a crisis! Confusion and division are rampant. Assurance of truth has surrendered to uncertainty. Surety of faith has given way to an enfeebling pluralism. Uniqueness has been overcome by ecumenicalism. The sense of urgency has been replaced by carnal security. The spiritual church has become a social club. Unwavering loyalty is now branded as bigotry. Faithfulness to Christ is judged legalism. The defenders of truth are spurned as schismatics. The state of the church has led untold thousands to reevaluate their relationship to it. This book addresses this issue of separation.

The Entertainment Syndrome (116 pages)

This book explores how the large increase in entertainment impacts the physical, emotional, social, intellectual and spiritual life of the human race, and the devastating effect of its use in our churches.

The European Union, the American Union, the Papacy, and Globalism

The book of Revelation reveals a powerful global movement just prior to the return of Christ—a moment which is deeply riveted in both politics and religion. They provide evidence that the Papacy is the religious backbone of this movement as it postures to become the superpower upon the planet. They explain the reason why this globalism will lead to the greatest tyranny this planet has ever witnessed and how every major unit of society will continue to support this globalism. The authors present evidence from biblical prophecy that this global thrust will not completely be achieved and how the world will be liberated from ruthless globalists.

The Evangelical Dilemma (222 pages)

There has never been a more urgent time for an honest review of the past, present and future of Evangelical Protestantism. The authors present an examination of the major doctrinal errors of Evangelical Protestants.

The Everlasting Gospel (368 pages)

This book is written for all sincere Christians of all faiths. The authors have been puzzled why so many Christians strongly believe "the gospel" and yet ignore the central theme of the gospel. The authors have preached this gospel on every inhabited continent of the world and now they present it in a fascinating, simply explained presentation in this book for all to understand and share with others.

The Gathering Storm and The Storm Burst (421 pages)

***The Gathering Storm* (Part 1)**—The Seventh-day Adventist Church experienced a tragic and dramatic redirection of its doctrines and practices beginning in the mid-1950s. While many were aware of this, few knew the almost unbelievable story behind this great apostasy. In this section, formerly entitled *Adventism Challenged A*, the authors have traced the only authentic, comprehensive development of this tragic area in God's remnant Church. Remarkably, God placed them in situations that allowed them to be eyewitnesses to the unfolding events. This book will challenge every reader who is loyal to Christ to rise up on behalf of God, His Word and His Truth.

***The Storm Burst* (Part 2)**—The ease with which previous heresies successfully invaded the Seventh-day Adventist Church had been of great shock to all faithful members. Though we have been warned constantly that it would happen, its reality has come as a whirlwind into our midst. *Adventism Challenged B* continues to detail how the new theology was imported from Australia to the United States and other parts of the world. The authors document the earnest efforts of many current leaders, former leaders, and laity, to stay the plague of unfaithfulness to the truth and mission of the SDA Church.

The General Conference Confronts Apostasy (640 pages)

While a number of excellent histories of the Seventh-day Adventist church have been written, *The General Conference Confronts Apostasy* is unique. No other historical volume has documented in detail the manner in which church leaders have dealt with apostasy in our midst from its earliest times. Commencing with fanatical worship services, moving to the Messenger and the Marian offshoots, then to the entry of what is now commonly known as the "new theology" with the defection of Pastor Dudley Canright, this book takes up the earth-shattering 1888 General Conference session, the promotion of pantheism, the "holy flesh" movement of Indiana in 1900, hierarchical church governance, the issue of self-supporting work, the military issue of World War I, and the trend-setting 1919 Bible conference. *The General Conference Confronts Apostasy* examines each one in detail, presenting the impact upon God's Church in the twenty-first century.

Georgia Sits On Grandpa's Knee (R. Standish) (86 pages)

World-traveler Russell Standish delights in visiting with his little grand-daughter, Georgia. She loves to sit on her grandpa's knee and hear stories of "the old times" when her daddy was a little boy in Australia, Malaysia, Thailand, England, and Singapore. And it is Dr. Standish's delight to also share these tales of a family era now past—the joys of life together in exotic lands. Georgia thinks that other children will enjoy her grandpa's stories. Grandpa hopes so, too!

God's Other Arm (106 pages)

Self-supporting ministries, independent ministries, supporting ministries—sometimes there seems to be utter confusion in the Seventh-day Adventist church today about their roles. Some church members believe that the denominational work is so paralyzed by apostasy, worldliness, and corruption that lay ministries are the only hope for finishing the gospel commission. Others militantly oppose lay ministries, labeling them schismatics, divisive, separationists, cultists, and offshoots.

***God's Solution for Depression, Guilt and Mental Illness* (229 pages)**

This powerful book argues with great persuasiveness that God is interested in every aspect of His created beings and that the perfect answers to man's needs are to be found in the Word of God.

***Grandpa, You're Back!* (R. Standish) (128 pages)**

Pastor Russell Standish again delights and fascinates his granddaughter, Georgia, with stories of his many travels to countries ranging from South America to such far-flung places as Singapore, Africa, and beyond. These stories should pleasantly awaken the imagination of young readers.

***The Greatest of All the Prophets* (411 pages)**

In 2004, under the guise of protecting the Spirit of Prophecy, the South Pacific Division launched an eight-pronged attack against the Testimonies of God. This book thoroughly documents the attack and the parallel defaming of Scripture. The claimed errors of Scripture and the Spirit of Prophecy are examined in detail and refuted. The book sets forth the inerrant, infallible character of God's inspired messages. It establishes our faith, essential for those who love and trust God and truly desire salvation. It sets forth and exposes the fearful sophistries which are deceiving God's people today. This is a book for every church leader, theologian, pastor, elder and member. It is a book for its time.

***Gwanpa and Nanny's Home* (R. Standish and Ella Rankin) (128 pages)**

"I am Ella Marie Rankin. I want to tell you about Gwanpa's and Nanny's home. But I have a problem! You see, I'm only three and I haven't yet learned to write. So, my Gwanpa is writing my story for me." So begins a book that Russell Standish wrote for his granddaughter.

***Half a Century of Apostasy* (480 pages)**

This book covers the grim harvest of the "new theology" during the years of 1956 to 2006. It is the Mount Carmel in God's Seventh-day Adventist Church today. The words of the prophet Elijah, destined to be translated, echo in our ears once more: "How long halt ye between two opinions? if the LORD be God, follow him: but if Baal, then follow him" (1 Kings 18:21). Never in any book, outside Scripture and the Spirit of Prophecy, has a volume been written which has set forth so clearly the manifest departure from God's pure truth by His Church. Each brief chapter is an urgent call for reform in the power of the Holy Spirit. It is the authors' prayer that this book will open the eyes of the spiritually blind and help to prepare the hearts of sincere believers as each prepares for translation.

Handbook for Lay and Self-Supporting Workers (255 pages)

This handbook provides essential information, guidance, and practical information to enhance the ministry of both new and experienced lay workers, written by men who have founded successful lay ministries. Their wealth of information will provide a strong platform for avoiding numerous pitfalls and gaining new insights into a Spirit-filled, soul-saving ministry.

Holy Relics or Revelation (300 pages)

Biblical archaeologists have gathered data with painstaking effort, and their work proves the accuracy of the Bible. Yet, mostly within a single decade, Ron Wyatt had sought out and claimed the most amazing biblical sites and relics. In this book, the Standish Brothers examine the Wyatt claims in-depth. Their findings serve as a benchmark upon which Ron Wyatt's "discoveries" can be more carefully evaluated.

Keepers of the Faith (240 pages)

As every wind of doctrine is marshaled against the church, more determined efforts are required to alert and warn of the dangers and errors that are now endemic in most congregations. In this book, the authors have attempted to identify and explain clearly the nature of many of these errors, and to document the clear truth as revealed by Inspiration. The book is especially directed to gospel ministers and lay leaders in the church. Previous editions of the book have found wide circulation among rank-and-file laity who discovered it to be one of the clearest presentations of biblical principles of truth and righteousness.

Liberty in the Balance (263 pages)

The bloodstained pathway to religious and civil liberty faces its greatest test in 200 years. The United States "Bill of Rights" lifted the concept of liberty far beyond the realm of toleration to an inalienable right for all citizens. Yet, for a century and a half, some students of the prophecies of John the Revelator have foretold a time just prior to the return of Christ when these most cherished freedoms will be wrenched from the citizens of the United States, and the U.S. would enforce its coercive edicts upon the rest of the world. This book traces the courageous battle for freedom, a battle stained with the lives of many martyrs.

The Lord's Day (310 pages)

In his famous encyclical *Dies Domini*, Pope John Paul II commenced with these words, "The Lord's Day—as Sunday was called from apostolic times. . . ." To many Protestants, this was an unexpected and much-approved declaration from the Roman Catholic supreme pontiff. The issue of the apostolic origin of Sunday-worship has often been a contentious one between Roman Catholics and Protestants. This book presents an in-depth examination of the Sabbath in the Scriptures.

Missionary To Jamaica (176 pages)

Nothing compares with foreign missionary service in a land far away from home and in a country whose culture is widely different from your own. Through this book you will "live" some of the joys, blessings, and miracles along with the frustrations, death threats, tragic experiences, and complex issues Colin and Cheryl Standish had to face. They will introduce you to a fascinating nation, culture, and vibrant people—a people they learned to love dearly and in so many ways to respect. This book is for those of all ages who love missionary stories.

Modern Bible Translations Unmasked **(228 pages); Supplement (30 pages)**

This fascinating book challenges the reader to consider two very serious problems with modern translations: first, the use of corrupted Greek manuscripts, and second, translational bias. The authors are deeply concerned about the paraphrases and some of the efforts to translate the Bible into colloquial language, but they are also deeply concerned about the more respected translations that are gaining great acceptance in today's society. You will learn how these modern translations are reinforcing false teachings and erroneous gospel presentations. The supplement contains Spirit of Prophecy quotations and other materials for Seventh-day Adventists on this important topic.

The Mystery of Death **(128 pages)**

There are those today who believe that the soul is immortal and externally preexisted the body. Pagan or Christian, the opinions vary widely. In this book, the history of these concepts is reviewed and the words of Scripture are investigated for a definitive and unchallengeable answer.

Organizational Structure and Apostasy **(164 pages)**

This new reprint of *The Temple Cleansed* specifically details the way the organizational structure of the SDA Church is being molded after the deadly hierarchal pattern of the world. Few understand the simple organizational pattern that God provided for His church at all denominational and local levels—therefore, few raise the alarm. The eyes of the discerning reader should be opened to the type of organization God will have in place when he cleanses His church. The human machinery will be swept aside.

Perfection **(45 pages)**

The Bible teaches perfection of character, not perfection of flesh or nature. This book helps the leader to fully understand the Bible's teaching of perfection of character in all of its aspects.

Perils of Ecumenism (416 pages)

The march of ecumenism seems unstoppable. From its humble roots after the first World War, with the formation of the Faith and Order Council at Edinburgh University, Scotland, and the Works and Labor Council at Oxford University, England, to the formation of the World Council of Churches in 1948 in Amsterdam, it has gained breathtaking momentum. The authors see the ecumenical movement as very clearly identified in Holy Scriptures as the movement devised by the arch-deceiver to beguile the inhabitants of the world.

Perils of Time Setting (82 pages)

This book demonstrates the failure of every time setting prediction ever made since 1844. It gives conclusive evidence that such time setting has its foundations in the Jesuit scheme to derail the Protestant Reformation and to refocus Protestants from their unwavering identification of the Papacy as the historical Antichrist of prophecy. It is an invaluable guide as to how to avoid being trapped by tantalizing but false principles of biblical interpretation.

The Pope's Letter and Sunday Laws (116 pages)

The authors examine the biblical foundations upon which the pope seeks to buttress his apostolic letter, *Dies Domini*. But even the undoubted skill of the pope and his scholarly advisors cannot mask the fallacies of the pope's conclusions. The authors show emphatically that the pope's assertions are in deep contradiction to the record of the Holy Bible and that of history.

Postmodernism and the Decline of Christianity

Like stealth in the night, postmodernism has not only invaded the world but the church. It is a concept in which there are no universal laws, no ultimates, no immutables. It is a belief which developed out of the modernist world, though it has gone far beyond modernism. It is based upon the feelings of each individual. Truth is nothing more than the whims of each individual. Few Christians have understood the postmodernist agenda, let alone the profound influence it has exerted upon the Christian church. This book exposes how far this influence has invaded the portals of the Christian establishments and how it is destroying the very fabric of society.

The Rapture and the Antichrist (288 pages)

This book sets forth the plainest truths of Scripture directing Protestantism back to its biblical roots. It will challenge the thinking of all Christians, erase the fictions of the *Left Behind* Series, and plant the reader's spiritual feet firmly on the platform of Scripture.

The Rapture, the End Times and the Millennium (378 pages)

This book will open the minds of the readers to a clear understanding of areas of the end-time which have led to much perplexity among laypeople and theologians alike. It is also guaranteed to dispel many of the perplexities presently confronting those who are searching for a clear biblical exposition of the last cataclysmic days in which we now live.

Reflections on Eight General Conference Sessions (112 pages)

A thirty-five year span can be a significant period in the history of any church, especially in the bewildering world in which we now live. How has God's chosen, remnant church fared during this period of earth's history? Most churches during the last thirty-five years in Christendom have taken very sharp turns toward ecumenism, Pentecostalism, Roman Catholicism, and worldly practices. How has our beloved church fared? This book examines the answer to this question through the evaluations of eight consecutive General Conference Sessions. Few delegates or visitors have attended eight consecutive General Conference sessions but one of the authors has. This review of the actions taken, messages presented, and the activities undertaken will be of deep interest to church members and church leaders alike.

The Road to Rome (217 pages)

Sister White wrote, "The Omega of Apostasy will be of a most startling nature." (*Selected Messages*, Vol. 1, pg. 197) She also stated—"The church has turned back from following Christ, her Leader, and is steadily retreating toward Egypt." (*Testimonies*, Vol. 1, pg. 217) The time is overdue for us to evaluate how far we have traveled down the Road To Rome! With deep sensitivity and a passionate love for their church, the authors have uncovered what many will recognize as an orchestrated plan to systematically implement the catholicizing of the Seventh-day Adventist Church.

The Sacrificial Priest (272 pages)

To all Christians the centrality of the sacrifice of Christ on Calvary has been the focus of their salvation hopes. However, relatively few Christians have understood the equally important ministry of Christ in the heavenly sanctuary. The authors provide a fascinating biblical explanation and irrefutable evidence of this little-studied high priestly ministry of Christ in the heavenly sanctuary.

The Second Coming (80 pages)

The Apostle Paul refers to the second coming of Jesus as the blessed hope. (Titus 2:12) Yet, soon after the death of all the apostles, doubts and debates robbed the people of this assurance and brought in the pagan notion of immediate life after death. In this new updated work, Colin and Russell Standish present a "wake-up call" for every complacent Christian.

The Sepulchres Are Whited (301 pages)

We are at the end of probationary time. If God's church is to receive the full outpouring of the latter rain, there must be a return to truth and righteousness. This alone will provide the unity that God can honor with His Spirit. This book is written to stimulate such a reformation in our ranks.

***Spiritism in the SDA Church* (133 pages)**

The authors believe that every deviation from truth has its root in spiritism. They take a broad concept of spiritism to include idolatry, paganism, humanism, New Age philosophy, Catholicism and Satanism, and explore some surprisingly "respectable" forms of spiritism that are designed especially for the more wary Christian. This book reveals the frightening inroads of spiritualistic theory and practice that has become deeply embedded within much of contemporary Seventh-day Adventism.

***Tithes and Offerings—Trampling The Conscience* (112 pages)**

With unreasonable fervor and scant knowledge, many have sought to condemn God's ordained self-supporting ministries that accept tithe for their soul saving gospel work. This has led the tithe issue to become a religious liberty issue in God's Church. This book is a remarkable contribution to our understanding of this topic. The authors have researched the tithe issue to a depth never before attempted, and have again done what they do best–bring an issue back to the objective evidence of God's sacred Word and the Spirit of Prophecy.

***Twenty-eight Fundamentals: Apostasy Proclaimed in Silence* (234 pages)**

Throughout the history of God's church on earth the insinuation of apostasy has been achieved, not so much in open pronouncements, but by guile and stealth. Silence has been the major weapon upon which error has comfortably rested. By subtlety it has found a foothold in God's church. Through this stratagem, the initial tolerance of both precious truth and damnable error, a channel has been opened so that sacred principles of faith and the destructive errors of Satan have been permitted, for a season, to lie together as bedfellows. This ploy has served the cause of Satan all too well. It has, in turn, led ultimately to the spurning of truth.

Two Beasts, Three Deadly Wounds and Fifteen Popes (234 pages)

Revelation 13 presents two incomprehensible beasts—one of which received a deadly wound in one of its heads. Prophecy stated that this mortal injury would be healed, and that the power represented by the beast would be admired worldwide. The authors give a detailed history of the fifteen popes who have sat upon the papal throne since the infliction of the deadly wound. The reader will find compelling evidence that the deadly wound is now so well-healed that there remains virtually no trace of the scar. For students of Scripture, this book will enlighten and bring an understanding of biblical prophecy and perhaps a new appreciation of the conclusive accuracy of Bible prophecy. The authors present this book as for all minds, a challenge to all hearts, and a timely wake-up call for humanity.

Uncle Russell and Daddy Stories (208 pages)

When Colin's children, Nigel and Alexandra, were growing up, he frequently told them stories and lessons gleaned from events in the life of Colin and his twin brother Russell during the time they were boys and youth growing up in Australia. These stories included the surprise birth of Colin and Russell, some of the challenges of the depression years, up to their college graduation. Although the stories are not always flattering to two boys born into a very poor but deeply dedicated family, they provide unique, first-hand insights into the happenings and events which were to lay the foundation for a lifetime of service for the Savior.

The Vision and God's Providences (C. Standish): Unabridged (240 pages); Abridged (176 pages)

The story of the development of Hartland Institute must be attributed to God alone. Yet, many men and women have had the privilege of being His humble instruments to contribute to Hartland's establishment. This book recalls divine leadings, human weakness, misunderstandings, and strong differences of opinion, and we cannot but wonder what God might have accomplished, had we listened perfectly to His voice.

***Why Members Leave the Seventh-day Adventist Church* (256 pages)**

The authors have developed a great concern for the terrible carnage of members in the Seventh-day Adventist Church. When they were children in Australia there was great concern because 30 percent of children born into the Seventh-day Adventist homes were choosing to walk away from the Church. However, several years ago they were staggered to learn that now 81 percent of the Church's youth were abandoning the Seventh-day Adventist Church in Australia and New Zealand. They also learned that an alarming number of members who had been added through evangelistic outreach soon thereafter walk away from the church. In this book the authors share the Divine solutions to the many different ways that Satan has found to achieve this deplorable situation.

***Winds of Doctrine* (174 pages)**

Satan has not confined his attacks to denominational workers and leaders, but has also attacked those in the self-supporting work. The tragedy is that some have accepted the nefarious subtleties of Satan and have led many that are not stabilized in the faith away from truth and righteousness. This book is essential reading for all earnest Seventh-day Adventists. It takes up the issues central to the apostasy—the name of God, the Godhead, the Person of the Holy Spirit, the eternal existence of Christ, the Wednesday crucifixion, the correct Sabbath hours, and God's destructive judgment.

***Youth, Are You Preparing for Your Divorce?* (168 pages)**

A majority of youth, including Christian youth, are destined for divorce. Yes, you read this correctly! Unbeknown to them or to their parents, long before marriage or even courtship, the seeds of divorce have been sown to later produce their baneful consequences. Many youth who think they are preparing for marital bliss are preparing for divorce and, all too frequently, their parents are co-conspirators in this tragedy. The authors provide amazing simple principles to avert the likelihood of future divorce.

***Youth Do You Dare!* (C. Standish) (88 pages)**

If you are a young person looking for workable answers to the many issues that confront you today, this book is for you. It presents a call to young people to follow truth and righteousness, and to live morally upright lives.

Other Books from Hartland Publications

***Behold the Lamb*—David Kang (107 pages)**

God's plan of redemption for this world and the preservation of the universe is revealed in the sanctuary which God constructed through Moses. This book explains the sanctuary service in the light of the Christian's personal experience. Why this book? Because Jesus is coming soon!

***China Letters*—David Lin (428 pages)**

Applies the hammer of truth to the tensile of New Theology, exposing the nature of the base metal for what really is, not gold or silver, but rather tin and dross. These collected letters and articles appeared in various Adventist periodicals at a time when Ford's teachings were the center of attention in the SDA church.

***Christ and Antichrist*—Samuel J. Cassels (348 pages)**

First published in 1846 by a well-known Presbyterian minister, who called this book "not sectarian, but a Christian and Protestant work." He hoped that the removal of obstacles might result in a more rapid spread of the Gospel. One of these obstacles he saw as "Antichristianity," a term he that he used to describe the Papal system.

***Distinctive Vegetarian Cuisine*—Sue M. Weir (329 pages)**

100% vegan cooking, with no animal products—no meat, milk, eggs, cheese, or even honey. No irritating spices or condiments are used. Most of the ingredients can be found at your local market. There are additional nutritional information and helpful hints. Make your dinner table appealing to the appetite!

***Food for Thought*—Susan Jen (160 pages)**

Where does the energy which food creates come from? What kinds of foods are the most conductive to robust health and well being in all dimensions of our life? What is a balanced diet? Written by a healthcare professional, this book examines the food we prepare for our table.

***Group Think*—Horace E. Walsh (96 pages)**

Find out how a state of groupthink (or group dynamics) has often contributed to disaster in secular and spiritual matters, like the role of Hebrew groupthink in the rejection and ultimate crucifixion of the Son of God. Or, the Ecumenical Movement that seeks to unite the minds of dedicated men so much that their passion is to build one great super church following Rome.

***Heroes of the Reformation*—Hagstotz and Hagstotz (320 pages)**

This volume brings together a comprehensive picture of the leaders of the Reformation who arose all over Europe. The authors of this volume have made a sincere endeavor to bring the men of Protestantism alive in the hearts of this generation.

***His Mighty Love*—Ralph Larson (159 pages)**

Twenty-one evangelistic sermons! Every doctrine of the Bible is simply an answer to the question, "How does the love of God relate to this particular question or problem?" Every doctrine is further evidence that God is love! This book is divided into three sections with seven individual sermons each. Subjects range from "If God Is Almighty, Why Does He Permit Sin?" to "The Unpardonable Sin."

***History of the Gunpowder Plot*—Philip Sidney (303 pages)**

Originally published on the 300th anniversary of the November 5, 1605, plot aimed at the destruction of the English Realm, is Philip Sydney's account of one of the most audacious conspiracies ever known to the ancient or modern. The failed plot became part of English popular culture.

***The History of Protestantism*—J. A. Wylie (2,136 pages)**

This book pulls back the divine curtain and reveals God's hand in the affairs of His church during the Protestant Reformation. Your heart will be stirred by the lives of Protestant heroes, and your mind captivated by God's simple means to counteract the intrigues of its enemies. As God's church faces the last days, this compelling book will appeal and will be a blessing to adults as well as children.

***History of the Reformation of the 16th Century*—J. d'Aubigné (1,472 pages)**

In history and in prophecy, the Word of God portrays the long continued conflict between truth and error. Today, we see an alarming lack of understanding in the Protestant Church concerning the cause and effect of the Reformation. This reprinted masterpiece pulls back the curtain of history and divine providence to reveal the true catalyst for the Reformation—God's Word and His Holy Spirit.

***History of the Reformation in the Time of Calvin*—d'Aubigné (1,971 pages)**

The renovation of the individual, of the Church, and of the human race, is the theme. This renovation is, at the same time, an enfranchisement; and we might assign, as a motto to the Reformation accomplished by Calvin, as well as to apostolic Christianity itself, these words of Jesus Christ: The truth shall make you free. (John 8:32)

***History of the Waldenses*—J. A. Wylie (191 pages)**

During the long centuries of papal supremacy, the Waldenses defied the crushing power of Rome and rejected its false doctrines and traditions. This stalwart people cherished and preserved the pure Word of God. It is fitting that this edition of their history should be reprinted to keep alive the spirit and knowledge of this ancient people.

***Hus the Heretic*—Poggius the Papist (78 pages)**

One of the greatest of Reformers in history was John Hus. His pious life and witness during his trial and martyrdom convinced many of the priests and church leaders of his innocence and the justice of his cause. Poggius was the papal legate who delivered the summons to Hus to appear at the council of Constance, then participated member. This book consists of letters from Poggius to his friend Nikolai, and describes the trial and burning of Hus. So potent was John Hus' humble testimony, that even some of his ardent foes became his defenders.

The Law and the Sabbath—Allen Walker (149 pages)

A fierce controversy is swirling around the role the Ten Commandments should play in the church of the 21st Century. With a foreword by the late Elder Joe Crews, here is a book that dares to examine the Bible's own answers—with unfailing scriptural logic and a profound appreciation for the doctrine of righteousness by faith.

The Method of Grace—John Flavel (458 pages)

In this faithful reprint, John Flavel thoroughly outlines the work of God's Spirit in applying the redemptive work of Christ to the believer. Readers will find their faith challenged and enriched. In true Puritan tradition, a clearly defined theology is delivered with evangelistic fervor, by an author urgently concerned about the eternal destiny of the human soul.

The Reformation in Spain—Thomas M'Crie (272 pages)

The boldness with which Luther attacked the abuses and the authority of the Church in Rome in the 16th Century attracted attention throughout Christendom. Luther's writings, along with the earlier ones of Erasmus, gained a foothold with a Spanish people hungry for the truth. Thomas M'Crie makes a case for a Spain free of the religious errors and corruptions that ultimately dried up the resources and poisoned the fountains of a great empire.

Romanism and the Reformation—H. Grattan Guinness (217 pages)

The Reformation of the 16th Century, which gave birth to Protestantism, was based on Scripture. It gave back to the world the

Bible. Such Reformation work needs to be done again today. The duty of diffusing information on the true character and history of "Romanism and the Reformation" is one that presses on God's faithful people in these days.

Strange Fire—Barry Harker (206 pages)

The Olympic games are almost universally accepted as a great international festival of peace, sportsmanship, and friendly competition. Yet, the games are riddled with conflict, cheating, and objectionable competitiveness. Discover the disturbing truth about the modern Olympics and the role of Christianity in the rise of this neo-pagan religion.

The Third Angel's Message of Righteousness by Faith and Its Present Rejection—L. Scarborough (107 pages)

As Seventh-day Adventists, we tend to believe that our greatest danger of being deceived by error would come from without the church. Our concerns have been concentrated upon these varied forms of deceptions. We are far less prepared to stand against the deceptions that will come from within our own church.

Truth Triumphant—Benjamin George Wilkinson (440 pages)

The prominence given to the "Church in the Wilderness" in the Scriptures establishes without argument its existence and emphasizes its importance. The same challenges exist today with the Remnant Church in its final controversy against the powers of evil to show the holy, unchanging message of the Bible.

Who Are These Three Angels?—Jeff Wehr (126 pages)

The messages of three holy angels unfold for us events that are soon to take place. Their warning is not to be taken lightly. They tell of political and religious movements that signal the soon return of Jesus.

***With Cloak and Dagger*—H. H. Meyers (160 pages)**

This is a startling revelation of a deliberate and successful effort by a small group of men to sabotage effectively the message and mission of God's remnant church. The basic fundamental principles that were endorsed by God's prophet to His remnant church as having "unquestionable authority," have since been systematically eroded and even changed!

***The Word Was Made Flesh*—Ralph Larson (365 pages)**

One hundred years of Seventh-day Adventist Christology, from 1852 to 1952. This book is a comprehensive survey of the historical evidence of the human nature of Christ. "The nature of God, whose law had been transgressed, and the nature of Adam, the transgressor, meet in Jesus, the Son of God, and the Son of Man." Ellen White, *Manuscript 141*, 1901.

***Youth Ministry in Crisis*—Barry Harker (206 pages)**

In this bracing book, Dr. Barry Harker examines the practices and passions that are transforming and debasing contemporary youth ministry—rock music, magic, clowning, comedy, drama, mime, puppetry, sports, extreme adventure activities, youth fashions and movies—and exposes the disturbing ideas that permit them to flourish in God's church. Dr. Harker also outlines steps that need to be taken if the enveloping crisis is to be resolved and youth ministry restored to a culture of defensible innovation. This book is a timely corrective to the ideas and practices that are defacing the image of God in His people.

True Education History Series from Hartland Publications

***Livingstone—The Pathfinder*—Basil Matthews (112 pages)**

Like most boys and girls, David Livingstone wondered what he would become when he grew up. He had heard of a brave man who was a missionary doctor in China. He also learned that this Dr. Gulztoff had a Hero, Jesus, who had come to people as a healer and missionary. David learned all about this great Physician, and felt that the finest thing in the whole world for him was to follow in the same way and be a medical missionary. That was David's quest, which was his plan. Between these pages, you shall see how he made his good wish come true.

***Missionary Annals—Memoir of Robert Moffat*—M. L. Wilder (64 pages)**

Robert Moffat first heard from his wise and pious mother's lips that there were heathen in the world and of the efforts of Christians sharing the knowledge of a Savior who could raise them out of their base degradation. An intense desire took possession of him to serve God in some marked manner but how that would be, he did not know. Through a series of providential circumstances and in God's good time, the London Society accepted him as one of their missionaries, and in 1816, he embarked on his first trip and got his first glimpse of heathen Africa. This book will inspire the young and old as you read the many trials, disappointments, triumphs, and wondrous miracles that God can accomplish when one is fully surrendered to Him.

***The Waldenses*—The Church in the Wilderness (72 pages)**

The faithful Waldenses in their mountain retreats were married in a spiritual sense to God who promised, "I will betroth thee unto me in faithfulness and thou shalt know the Lord." (Hosea 2:20) No invention of Satan could destroy their union with God. Follow the history of these people as they are compared to the dedicated eagle parents.

Meet the Author

Colin Standish

COLIN D. STANDISH was born in Newcastle, Australia, in 1933, a twin in a family of four children. He attended college and completed his Bachelor of Arts in psychology, with honors, at the University of Sydney. Colin completed his Master of Arts and Doctor of Philosophy, both in psychology, and then a second Master's in education.

Dr. Standish is currently president and pioneer of Hartland Institute in Rapidan, Virginia, which comprises a college, a wellness center, publishing house and a world mission division. Previously, he taught in the psychology department of the University of Sydney, and chaired the education department of Avondale College, Australia. He served as academic dean and president of West Indies College, Jamaica, and also as chairman of the psychology department, academic dean, and president of Columbia Union College, Maryland. He also served as dean of Weimar College, California.

He is the author of numerous books on Christian living. He enjoys music, nature, and spending time with his wife, Cheryl, and two children, Nigel and Alexandra. He has an enormous burden to help young people succeed mentally, spiritually and physically.

HARTLAND Publications was established in 1984 as a Bible-centered, self-supporting Protestant publishing house. We publish Bible-based books and produce media for Christians of all ages, to help them in the development of their personal characters, always giving glory to God in preparation for the soon return of our Lord and Savior, Christ Jesus. We are especially dedicated to reprinting significant books on Protestant history that might otherwise go out of circulation. Hartland Publications supports and promotes other Christian publishers and media producers who are consistent with biblical principles of truth and righteousness. We are seeking to arouse the spirit of true Protestantism, one that is based on the Bible and the Bible only, thus awakening the world to a sense of the value and privilege of the religious liberty that we currently enjoy.

Office hours (Eastern time):
Monday – Thursday: 9:00 a.m. to 5:00 p.m.
Friday: 9:00 a.m. to 12:00 noon

Payment must be in US dollars by check, money order, or most credit cards.

You may order via mail, telephone, fax, e-mail, or on the web site:

Hartland Publications
PO Box 1, Rapidan, VA 22733 USA

Order line: 1-800-774-3566 / Fax: 1-540-672-3568
E-mail: sales@hartlandpublications.org
Web site: www.hartlandpublications.com